WORDPRESS

PLUGINS

690 Free WordPress Plugins for Developing

Amazing and Profitable Websites

~2018 Edition~

Chad Tennant

*****

Links to sources and references can be accessed directly from the e-book edition. The e-book is downloadable free of charge with the purchase of the paperback edition.

Remember to backup your website/database regularly, and before installing any plugins as a best practice and security precaution.

Contents

INTRODUCTION

In 2009, I required a website designer for a financial blog I was starting. I didn't have a clue how to set up a website, so I hired someone in my network. After the creation of three sample sites and mounting expenses, I learned how to create websites, which has become an invaluable skill. The designer used WordPress, so I started to learn more about it. Nine years later, I've created many websites—some good and some bad—and I've enjoyed evolving with WordPress. It's easy to use, yet amazingly powerful and practical. Furthermore, I still don't know or need to know how to code because WordPress does most of the heavy lifting.

If I've learned anything, the ability to create websites quickly is an extremely important tech-business skill to possess. Knowing how to design and develop a functional website provides endless self-employment, entrepreneurial, and side hustle opportunities.

WordPress is a free open-source software and content management system (CMS). Users can access thousands of free and paid themes and plugins to develop their websites. A theme is a website template and framework that can be customized by its user. A plugin extends the functionality of a website in any number of categories including security, image management, search engine optimization, social media and so on.

WordPress powers 29 percent of all websites and leads the way in content management systems with a market share of 60 percent. You can visit Wikipedia for more details.

With <u>53,000</u> plus plugins and growing, there are many to choose from and everyone has their favorites. Deciding on which plugins to use is very much a trial, error, and fun experiment. However, I have tracked down the best free plugins in over thirty different categories since no such listed existed. I searched high and low and page after  page to bring you the best of the best.

Many articles address the "best," "must have," and "top" plugins, but none of them are as comprehensive as my list. This book is your ultimate reference guide. The list of 665 plugins represents roughly 1.25 percent of all plugins available.

Have fun exploring these plugins and building profitable websites.

To your success!

Chad Tennant, WordPress Enthusiast

8

WORDPRESS.ORG VS. WORDPRESS.COM

There can be some confusion between WordPress.org and WordPress.com, so let's understand their differences.

WordPress.org

WordPress.org provides free open-source software to run a website, blog, or app. It acts as an information repository for all things WordPress. You will find plenty of information and resources regarding themes, plugins, documentation, and support.

In tandem with the free open-source software, you'll need a hosting provider—the company that will keep your website up and running on the internet. WordPress.org recommends DreamHost (the provider I use), Bluehost, and SiteGround. However, thousands of hosting providers exist. Hosting usually cost around ten dollars a month depending on the provider. Furthermore, you can purchase and renew a domain name for about ten to fifteen dollars annually. For instance, www.yourdomain.com. With DreamHost, as well as many other service providers, the installation of WordPress software is achieved through an efficient one-click installation process.

The open-source environment of WordPress.org attracts thousands of developers who create free themes and plugins for everyone to use. This yields a lot of selection, but user support can be hit or miss depending on the developer.

WordPress.com

WordPress.com offers WordPress software, hosting, support, and limited themes and plugins all in one place. It's a one-stop-shop managed by Automattic—a website development company. The founder of Automattic, Matt Mullenweg, is also the founder of the WordPress software and foundation that runs WordPress.org.

WordPress.com controls the themes and plugins users have access to, so the selection is limited. Also, you can't add plugins from this book to your site since you won't find a "plugins tab" on your WordPress.com dashboard. WordPress.com offers just over 300 themes, which pales in comparison to the thousands of themes available on WordPress.org. However, WordPress.com's assortment of themes and plugins satisfy most customers. Automattic manages technical issues, and they offer excellent customer support.

You can get a free website at WordPress.com, if you don't mind using an address like yourname.wordpress.com, but you aren't likely to show up in search engine results. For a custom domain name, you'll have to pay.

Which Is Better?

WordPress.com is ideal for people who want convenience and support, but don't mind operating in a closed environment with fewer theme and plugin options. WordPress.org is ideal for individuals who want greater control and options for their sites, but with less support.

I recommend choosing WordPress.org because so much more is available, for example, themes, plugins, customization, security, and so on.

WORDPRESS COMMUNITY

Thousands of WordPress users flock to WordPress.org for support. However, support and social interactions are available on other websites and face-to-face.

Facebook

There are many WordPress themed Facebook groups. Some groups allow members to discuss all things WordPress compared with groups that focus on particular topics. For example, a group that discusses plugins only. To avoid getting banned, it's critical to understand the group's rules and guidelines before posting or commenting.

To find WordPress groups on Facebook, type "WordPress" in the Facebook search bar then select the "Groups" tab. I join groups that have a minimum of five thousand members and an engaged administrator who controls spam. See this post for the fifteen best Facebook groups for WordPress users.

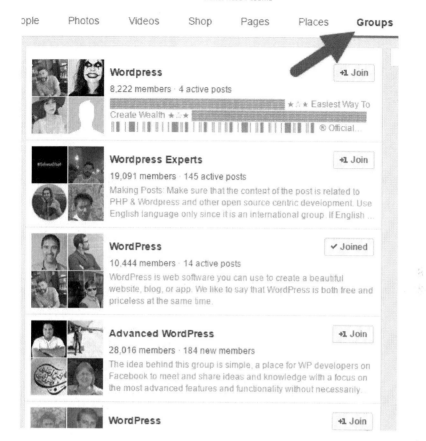

WordCamp

WordCamps are casual, locally-organized conferences covering WordPress. WordCamps include sessions on how to optimize WordPress, advanced techniques, security, and more. WordCamps are attended by bloggers, developers, website designers, and consultants. WordCamps combine scheduled programming with conference sessions and other activities. To get an idea of the WordCamp experience, check out the WordCamp channel at WordPress.tv.

WORDPRESS TRAINING

WordPress is super easy to use since it doesn't require extensive knowledge regarding coding or web development. The WordPress framework makes developing and managing websites straightforward. However, there is tremendous value in learning about the intricacies of WordPress. A new WordPress user should consider taking a beginner's course to save him or herself from wasteful trial, error, and frustration. As an experienced WordPress user, I occasionally watch tutorials on YouTube to learn and problem solve.

There are plenty of free e-learning websites and online resources with Codex—WordPress's information support library—leading the way. YouTube is another fantastic option to watch how-to videos. For example, how to design a WordPress website.

WordPress Blogs

There are dozens of WordPress authority sites covering news, reviews, tips, tricks, and tutorials. I visit some of them from time to time as an alternative to YouTube. Elegant Themes (Divi/Bloom) has a list of twenty-two WordPress blogs worth reading. Furthermore, you can visit these top ranked sites for WordPress tips, insights, and more.

- Elegant Themes
- WPBeginner
- WPExplorer
- WPMudev
- ManageWP
- WPKube

FREE AND PAID PLUGINS AND THEMES

With thousands of free plugins and themes available, why would anyone pay for either? Most of the time free plugins/themes will suffice, but sometimes they won't. Sometimes "free" can only take you so far or not far enough. Moreover, you may want features such as analytics, customer support, and customization, which free plugins often lack. For instance, if growing your email list is a priority, you'll want a robust opt-in form plugin to achieve desired results. While there are several free popup plugins, their features are limited. I wasn't content after trying a couple of these free plugins, so I purchased Bloom by Elegant Themes. So far, so awesome!

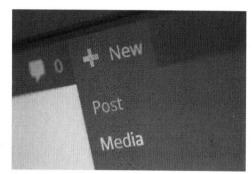

Many premium plugins and themes cost between twenty to one-hundred dollars and these costs can add up quickly without a game plan. When considering which free or paid plugins/themes to use, I recommend taking the following steps:

1. Before beginning your search for a plugin or theme, put on your project manager's hat and define your requirements. Consider and predetermine your objectives, needs, and priorities for your website. Your thoughts and ideas don't need to be concrete, but it helps to start from a place of knowingness and objectivity.
2. Search for free plugins/themes within your WordPress dashboard and select four to six contenders. Install, activate, and evaluate them against your requirements. Narrow down your list to two selections and explore them further. If they don't meet your needs, repeat this step or consider searching for paid plugins/themes on the internet. If you take the latter step, purchase one theme at a time and experiment. If all else fails, review your requirements and make any necessary adjustments so that you can find a plugin/theme that meets your needs.
3. Review your requirements on an ongoing basis and if things change, repeat steps one and two.

General Public License (GPLv2)

"The licenses for most software are designed to take away your freedom to share and change it. By contrast, the GNU General Public License is intended to guarantee your freedom to share and change free software—to make sure the software is free for all its users. This General Public License applies to most of the Free Software Foundation's software and to any other program whose authors commit to using it." –WordPress.org

Only recently did I engage in a debate about free versus paid plugins/themes in a Facebook group. It appears there are some hardcore WordPress users who believe paid solutions have no place in the open-source WordPress environment.

WordPress is an excellent platform, and users can find many exceptional free plugins/themes. However, WordPress also offers business opportunities for web designers and developers who want to make money—I think they call this capitalism.

I'm glad I don't have to pay for every single plugin I use, but I'm happy to invest in my online business through premium plugins and themes that improve my website. GPL hippies must get over themselves and appreciate entrepreneurs seeking to deliver premium products that outperform free ones. People have bills to pay, and I appreciate developers who want to deliver game-changing products. If their solutions are worthwhile, they'll succeed. If their products suck, they'll fail.

TOP FIVE PREMIUM PLUGINS

I love free plugins, and of the twenty-something plugins I use, all but two are paid—Bloom and Thrive Themes. I strongly believe that one or two premium plugins can make a huge difference.

Premium plugins attract fees for a reason, and usually it's because they offer more than their free counterparts, for example, amazing features or customer support. My recommendation is to experiment with free plugins until you've run out of options, want more, and can justify the cost. For instance, I tried SumoMe and MailMunch before implementing Bloom for list building and lead generation activities.

1. Thrive Themes

Thrive Themes offers a suite of marketing and lead capture plugins including opt-in forms, landing pages, countdown timers, and more. Users get various list building and marketing solutions at affordable prices. Thrive Themes offers:

- Thrive Leads: eleven types of opt-in forms including scroll mat, ribbon, screen filler, content lock, footer, and more.
- Thrive Landing Pages: over 200 high converting sales, registration, and webinar pages.
- Content Builder: the fastest and most intuitive visual editor for WordPress. Easily create drag-and-drop layouts, add buttons, and elements.
- WordPress themes: several high-converting and responsive themes.
- Additional plugins including Clever Widgets, Headline Optimizer, Thrive Ultimatum, Thrive Ovation, Thrive Quiz Builder, and Thrive Comments

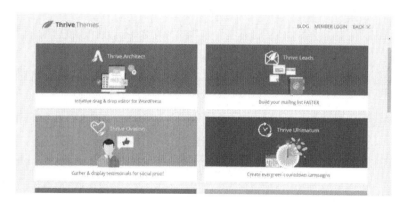

2. Elegant Themes

Divi is a very popular premium WordPress theme, plugin, and visual drag and drop page builder. The Bloom plugin is an excellent alternative to Thrive Leads for lead capture and list building activities. I use Bloom to create opt-in form in minutes.

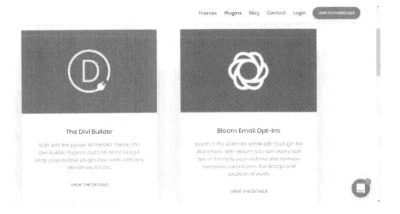

3. WP Rocket

Caching is the best way to reduce your site's loading time. You can speed up your WordPress website easily and quickly with the WP Rocket caching plugin. Visit their features page to see how they compare against free plugins.

4. iThemes

iThemes offers backup, maintenance, and security plugins. Since 2008, they've been creating tools to help people and businesses do more with WordPress.

- Backupbuddy: Make a complete backup of your entire WordPress site including the WordPress database, all files, settings, your WordPress themes and plugins, and more.
- iThemes Security Pro: Includes a one-click WordPress Security Check to enable recommended WordPress security settings so you don't have to configure everything manually.
- iThemes Sync Pro: Your personal WordPress website assistant. Instead of logging in to multiple websites, you can manage them all from one place.

5. ManageWP

Managing WordPress websites is a horrendous waste of time and energy, and it only gets worse as your business keeps scaling. Manage a bunch of websites for free, or make your life easier with premium add-ons. Keep the cost down with their flexible pricing model.

HOW MANY PLUGINS ARE TOO MANY?

It's easy to go crazy with adding plugins to our sites, but how many is too many? According to Dan Norris of WP Curve, "As a general guide, we like to keep sites to under 20 plugins. A better rule of thumb is 'less is best.' If you can have zero, then that's fantastic but probably unrealistic. We have two recommendations here: remove any plugins you don't need and remove any inactive or active plugins that you don't need." I have around twenty-five installed on chadtennant.com, and every plugin serves a measurable purpose.

Between Dan and I, we might agree that having twenty to thirty plugins is enough to achieve desired goals. However, having fifty-three or 637 plugins are also possibilities.

Plugins impact site performance in two distinct ways: additional HTTP requests and additional database queries, which ultimately influence factors such a website performance, page speed and loading times, security, and vulnerabilities associated with poorly coded or out-of-date plugins.

SPEED UP YOUR WORDPRESS SITE

Page speed is a measurement of how fast the content on your page loads. I had obsessed about my page speed until I got a high enough score on Google PageSpeed Insights (GPSI). Knowing that page speed is a Google search ranking factor, I check my score periodically and make changes if needed.

Page Speed Analyzers

The first step to increasing your page speed is to understand which areas of your website you need to improve. There are multiple page speed diagnostics tools that you can use, but GPSI should be your primary focus.

Google PageSpeed Insights measures the performance of a page for mobile and desktop devices. It fetches your URL twice, once with a mobile user-agent, and once with a desktop user-agent. Other page speed graders borrow at least some of their methodologies from GPSI. Here are a few common sites:

- Google PageSpeed Insights
- Think with Google
- Google Mobile-Friendly Test
- GTmetrix
- Pingdom
- Website Grader

What's a Good Score?

After you input and submit your URL into GSPI, you'll get a score and performance details. Starting with your score, Google says:

The PageSpeed Score ranges from 0 to 100 points. A higher score is better, and a score of 85 or above indicates that the page is performing well.

Eighty-five or above should be your aim or at the very least a score of seventy. Since page speed is just one of 200 factors Google uses in their ranking algorithm, you shouldn't necessarily forego other objectives just to achieve a high score. For example, using pop-ups to collect email addresses might be important to you, but they can negatively impact page speed scoring.

PageSpeed Insights

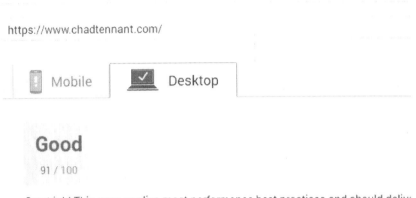

https://www.chadtennant.com/

Mobile ☑ Desktop

Good

91 / 100

Great job! This page applies most performance best practices and should deliv

⚠ **Possible Optimizations**

Eliminate render-blocking JavaScript and CSS in above-the-fold content

The performance details that will often appear in the "possible optimizations" are as follows and accompanied by the free WordPress plugin(s) that can rectify the issue. Also, I use and recommend WP Fastest Cache as an all-in-one plugin to boost scores.

Possible Optimizations

- "Eliminate render-blocking JavaScript and CSS in above-the-fold content" – Async JS and CSS / Autoptimize

- "Enable compression" – GZip Ninja Speed Compression

- "Leverage browser caching" – W3 Total Cache / WP Fastest Cache

- "Minify Javascript, CSS, HTML" – Better WordPress Minify

- "Optimize images" – ShortPixel Image Optimizer / WP SmushIt

- "Reduce server response time" – Autoptimize

Other Helpful Plugins

- Far Future Expiry Header
- JCH Optimize
- WordPress Gzip Compression
- WP Performance Score Booster
- WP Super Simple Speed

Other Considerations

You should fully understand page speed issues before attempting to fix them with plugins. There might be other actions you can take to speed up your site.

Installing a top-rated cache plugin and correctly setting it up can significantly improve your score. Cache plays a significant role in page speed performance.

WordPress themes can influence scores considerably. Some themes score poorly because of how they are designed and developed. If you use a clunky and inefficient theme, you may want to change it.

Plugins may have conflicts with other plugins. This happened to me when I installed Autoptimize, so I removed it. Also, to understand the impact of plugins on your site, the P3 plugin by GoDaddy is helpful.

The "Eliminate render-blocking" message can be caused by using a pop-up that occurs above-the-fold on a page or post, e.g., a scroll mat opt-in form. As previously mentioned, you must decide what's important to you, for instance, your page speed score or collecting email addresses.

Finding the correct combination of page performance plugins might take some experimentation, but it's worth it to improve a visitor's interaction with your website. On a related note, Google is laser-focused on mobile performance with initiatives such as the Accelerated Mobile Pages (AMP) project. You can find videos on my YouTube channel about this and the information above.

SECURE YOUR WORDPRESS SITE

Not a day goes by without breaking news of a major hack. WordPress is designed to thwart hacks, but other measures are needed to ensure optimal security.

- Install a top-rated security plugin, for example Wordfence, and review/update the settings.
- Change your login permalink. Many hackers try to login to sites. One place they attempt to get access is yoursite.com/**wp-login.php**, which is the default login permalink. Rename wp-login.php is a very light plugin that lets you easily and safely change wp-login.php to anything you want. It doesn't literally rename or change core files or add/rewrite rules. It simply intercepts page requests and works on any WordPress website. The wp-admin directory and wp-login.php page become inaccessible, so you should bookmark the URL. Deactivating the plugin returns your site to the way it was.
- Use trusted plugins and keep them updated to reduce vulnerabilities. Trusted plugins are those with excellent reviews and that are frequently updated. According to Sucuri, 56 percent of the hacked WordPress sites they analyzed were running out-of-date software. For example, Mossack Fonseca (MF), the Panamanian law firm at the center of the so-called Panama Papers Breach may have been breached via a vulnerable version of Revolution Slider. Elegant Themes gives advice on how to safely update plugins and how to address vulnerabilities.

- Get SSL for your site. You've probably noticed sites with "https" compared with "http." The sites with the former have an extra layer of security known as Secure Sockets Layer or SSL. SSL establishes an encrypted link between your web server and your visitor's web browser. This ensures that all data passed between the two remains private and secure. SSL is also a search engine ranking factor because it projects security and trust, which are the types of sites Alphabet (Google) and Microsoft (Bing) want to send visitors. Converting to SSL can be a free and easy process (you don't need to pay big bucks to companies like Norton). This article discusses the process in detail.

SEARCH ENGINE OPTIMIZATION (SEO)

Search engine optimization (SEO), you know what it is or are familiar with the concept, but is learning about it important to you?

I follow a simple mantra, **if nobody can see or find you, nobody will visit you**. In other words, if your posts, products, and services show up on the ninth page of Google search engine results, it will be difficult to attract visitors to your website and no/low traffic yields no/low sales. Therefore, understanding and implementing SEO activities is critical to attracting more visitors and sales.

Many studies highlight the importance of being on the first page of search engine results. Call it convenience or laziness, most people limit their clicks to page one results. According to Philip Petrescu, "On average, 71.33% of searches result in a page one organic click. Page two and three get only 5.59% of the clicks. On the first page alone, the first five results account for 67.60% of all the clicks and the results from 6 to 10 account for only 3.73%."

Learning about SEO and applying best practices won't guarantee top rankings. However, it will provide you with strategic advantages and allow you to pick SEO battles more wisely. For example, I've chosen not to write about certain topics because those posts would not likely rank well given existing results.

Who Should Learn SEO

Although SEO is just one of many online marketing activities, it's one of the most critical to learn. SEO obviously helps with search engine rankings, but it also helps with ranking wherever search is applicable. For example, on YouTube, Amazon, and Facebook. You should learn SEO if you:

- Own or manage a website or blog
- Conduct internet marketing activities like affiliate, content, social media, and video marketing
- Generate revenue through online marketplaces such as Amazon, eBay, Fiverr, and Upwork
- Appreciate SEO/SEM as part of your digital marketing strategy

SEO Training

Your goal should be to understand and implement robust SEO strategies. Taking too many courses won't lead to a greater understanding because the law of diminishing return will set in and vital points will become redundant. I recommend taking one or two courses and referring to a handful of resources. In a quest to learn SEO, a person can get overwhelmed by search results (the irony). Fortunately, my exposure to e-learning enables me to point you in the right direction.

- Coursera provides access to the world's best education by partnering with top universities and organizations to offer courses online. They've partnered with Stanford, Yale, and Princeton to name a few. Students can take courses for free or pay to obtain course completion certificates. Furthermore, Coursera offers specializations in various subjects. Moz started in 2004 as an SEO consultancy and expanded in the same direction to offer a range of software as a service (SaaS) solutions. Their brand has become synonymous with SEO, and they're considered a global authority. In fact, a search for "what is SEO" yields two Moz results on page one—that's walking the walking.

- Moz offers a treasure chest of online learning resources including guides, webinars (Mozinars), quizzes, whitepapers, and more. I explored several of their resources, which proved to be beneficial.
- While Moz is synonymous with SEO, Google is synonymous with search. Google commands nearly two-thirds of US search activity, and they have an incredible global brand. Millions of online users prefer Google over their chief rivals, for example, Bing and Yahoo. Suffice it to say; most training resources structure their contents based on Google's search engine, algorithms, and announcements. Google doesn't offer an SEO training course per se, but their brief SEO starter guide is a must-read. I recommend reading it after you learn a few things about SEO. Google offers free training for their various tools and platforms on websites such as YouTube.
- SearchEngineJournal (SEJ) is my favorite topical website. They publish insightful articles like "The Death of Organic Search (As We Know It)" and other content relating to online marketing. They offer a beginner's guide to SEO.
- HubSpot provides an outline on how to teach yourself SEO in thirty days.

There are several excellent WordPress SEO plugins including All-In-One-SEO and Yoast, but unless you understand SEO, these plugins **will be mostly useless**. Yoast has an academy consisting of a blog, e-books, and courses. Also, their YouTube channel is worth exploring.

SEO Website Analyzers

SEO website analyzers provide insights regarding a site's SEO performance. Hubspot has an analyzer and mentions several others in a post. SEO Site Checkup is also worth trying.

BEST FREE IMAGE WEBSITES

Since the early days of blogging, free images have been in high demand. There was a time when excellent free images were hard to procure, but in recent years hundreds of free image sites have surfaced. Whenever using images that aren't yours, it's vital that you understand the rights to avoid copyright infringement and fines.

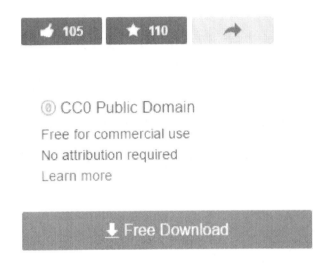

Hubspot has a list of the "20 of the Best Websites to Download Royalty-Free Stock Images." Some of the sites I use made their list including Pixabay, Picjumbo, and Gratisography.

Videos '

Along with images, I add videos from YouTube to my posts and pages. To add a video, I copy the embed link then paste it on a page/post. There are several free video plugins that help with embedding videos, but they aren't necessary.

JOB SITES AND MAKING MONEY

Some of you reading this book may be job hunting. There are several places you can look for web design/development opportunities as per below. LinkedIn, and your network can also assist with your job search activities.

- 99Designs
- Behance
- Coroflot
- Dribbble Jobs
- Envato
- Fiverr
- Freelancer
- Guru
- Problogger
- Smashing Jobs
- We Work Remotely
- WordPress.com
- WordPress.net
- WPHired
- Upwork

Make Money with WordPress

The WordPress ecosystem in wide and provides many monetization opportunities. For instance, I generate income from ads on my blog, ad revenue from WordPress tutorials on YouTube, books, and performance marketing. This article highlights thirty ways to make money with WordPress as a writer, marketer, consultant, instructor, salesperson, developer, and more. For example:

- Freelance Writer covering WordPress
- Hosting Provider
- Premium Plugin Developer
- Premium Theme Designer
- WordPress Blogger
- WordPress Consultant
- WordPress E-Commerce Retailer
- WordPress Fiverr Seller
- WordPress Online Instructor
- WordPress Page Speed Consultant
- WordPress SEO Consultant
- WordPress Website Developer

THE 690 BEST FREE PLUGINS

In the previous version of this book, I listed the top 665 free plugins. Now you have 690 at your disposal. To make the list, a plugin required a minimum of 30,000 active installs, ten reviews, and a four-star rating.

In a moment, you're going to sift through many amazing plugins. As any seasoned WordPress user knows, some plugin categories are more critical than others. For example, website administration, backup, SEO, and security categories should be top-of-mind regarding your site.

Although not highlighted in traditional hyperlink blue, plugins listed are clickable and will take you to the plugin's homepage on WordPress.org. I left the grammar as is regarding plugin titles and descriptions, so you will find plenty of grammatical errors. I did this to help with locating plugins of interest.

Ad Insert & Management Plugins (8)

Quick AdSense  Clickable Hyperlink

Quick AdSense offers a quicker & flexible way to insert Google AdSense or any Ads.

AdRotate

The popular choice for monetizing your website with adverts while keeping things simple.

Ad Inserter

Insert any advert or code into WordPress. Perfect for all kinds of banners and ads

AdSense Plugin WP QUADS

Quick Adsense Reloaded! Quickest way to insert Google AdSense & other ads into your website.

Ad Injection

Injects any adverts (e.g. AdSense) into the WordPress posts or widget area. Restrict who sees

Website Monetization by MageNet

Get additional income from your website or blog by placing text ads automatically.

Advanced Ads

Manage and optimize your ads and ads performance with support for AdSense, ad injection, ad

Wp-Insert

The Ultimate Adsense / Ad-Management Plugin for WordPress

Analytics & Statistics Plugins (15)

Google Analytics for WordPress by MonsterInsights

★★★★☆ (499)

The best Google Analytics plugin for WordPress. See how visitors find and use your website,...

 MonsterInsights

 1+ million active installations Tested with 4.9.0

Google Analytics for WordPress by MonsterInsights

The best Google Analytics plugin for WordPress.

Google Analytics Dashboard for WP

Displays Google Analytics stats in your WordPress Dashboard.

WP Statistics

Complete statistics for your WordPress site.

StatCounter – Free Real Time Visitor Stats

StatCounter.com powered real-time detailed stats about the visitors to your blog.

WP-PostViews

Enables you to display how many times a post/page had been viewed.

Slim Stat Analytics

Slim Stat Analytics

Count per Day

Visit Counter, shows reads and visitors per page, visitors today, yesterday, last week, last months.

WP-Piwik

This plugin adds a Piwik stats site to your WordPress or WordPress multisite dashboard.

Google Analytics Counter Tracker

Google analytics counter tracker – analyse the visitors hits on you website and display it.

NewStatPress

NewStatPress (Statpress plugin fork) is a real-time plugin to manage the visits' statistics about your.

Analytics

Analytics of Google: analytics code integration on WordPress website

Post Views Counter

Post Views Counter allows you to display how many times a post, page or custom

GA Google Analytics

Adds your Google Analytics Tracking Code to your WordPress site.

Visitors Traffic Real Time Statistics

Best statistics plugin for WordPress to display your site statistics & traffic. Enable you to

Statify

Visitor statistics for WordPress with focus on data protection, transparency and clarity. Perfect as a

Backup Plugins (10)

UpdraftPlus WordPress Backup Plugin

UpdraftPlus simplifies backups (and restoration). Backup into the cloud (Amazon S3 (or compatible), Dropbox, Google Drive, Rackspace Cloud, DreamObjects, FTP, Openstack Swift, UpdraftPlus Vault and email) and restore with a single click.

Duplicator

Duplicate, clone, backup, move and transfer an entire site from one location to another.

BackWPup – WordPress Backup Plugin

The backup plugin BackWPup can be used to save your complete installation including /wp-content/ and push them to an external Backup Service, like Dropbox, S3, FTP and many more, see list below.

WP-DB-Backup

On-demand backup of your WordPress database.

BackUpWordPress

Simple automated backups of your WordPress-powered website.

Backup Guard – backup & restore

Backup, clone, migrate, duplicate and restore your website.

XCloner – Backup and Restore

Backup your site, restore to any web location, send your backups to Dropbox, Amazon S3.

WP Database Backup

Create & Restore Database Backup easily on single click. Manual or automated backups (backup to.

Backup & Restore Dropbox

Backup & Restore Dropbox Plugin to create Dropbox Full Backup (Files + Database) or Restore,

Backup & Restore WPBackItUp

Backup, restore, clone, duplicate or migrate your site effortlessly with WPBackItUp.

Cache Plugins (Website Speed) (9)

WP Super Cache
★★★★☆ (1,309)

A very fast caching engine for WordPress that produces static html files.

Automattic

1+ million active installations Tested with 4.8.4

WP Super Cache

A very fast caching engine for WordPress that produces static html files.

W3 Total Cache

W3 Total Cache improves the SEO and user experience of your site by increasing website performance, reducing download times via features like content delivery network (CDN) integration.

WP Fastest Cache

The simplest and fastest WP Cache system.

LiteSpeed Cache

varnish, litespeed web server, lsws, availability, pagespeed, woocommerce, bbpress, nextgengallery, wp-polls, wptouch, customization, plugin, rewrite.

Varnish HTTP Purge

Automatically purge Varnish Cache when content on your site is modified.

DB Cache Reloaded Fix

The fastest cache engine for WordPress, that produces cache of database queries with easy configuration.

Nginx Helper

Cleans nginx's fastcgi/proxy cache or redis-cache whenever a post is edited/published. Also does a few

Hyper Cache

Hyper Cache is a performant and easy to configure cache system for WordPress.

Cache Enabler – WordPress Cache

A lightweight caching plugin for WordPress that makes your website faster by generating static HTML

Calendar & Event Plugins (11)

The Events Calendar

 (1,495)

The Events Calendar is a carefully crafted, extensible plugin that lets you easily share your...

 Modern Tribe, Inc.

 600,000+ active installations  Tested with 4.9.1

The Events Calendar

Create and manage your calendar of events with ease.

All-in-One Event Calendar

Calendar, ical, iCalendar, all-in-one, events sync, events widget, calendar widget.

Events Manager

Fully featured event registration management including recurring events, locations management, calendar, Google map integration, and more.

Comet Cache

Comet Cache is an advanced WordPress caching plugin inspired by simplicity.

Editorial Calendar

The Editorial Calendar makes it possible to see all your posts and drag and drop.

Event Organiser

Create and maintain events, including complex reoccurring patterns, venue management (with Google maps), calendars and

Booking Calendar

Booking Calendar plugin – is the ultimate booking system for online reservation and availability checking

Calendar by WD – Responsive Event Calendar for WordPress

Event Calendar plugin is a highly configurable product which allows you to have multiple organized

My Calendar

Accessible WordPress event calendar plugin. Show events from multiple calendars on pages, in posts, or

wp-jalali

Full Jalali calendar support for WordPress and localization improvements for Persian/Afghan/Tajik users.

Event Calendar WD – Responsive Event Calendar plugin

Event Calendar WD is a user-friendly event calendar plugin. This event calendar plugin allows organizing

CAPTCHA Plugins (6)

Really Simple CAPTCHA

★★★★½ (116)

Really Simple CAPTCHA is a CAPTCHA module intended to be called from other plugins. It...

Takayuki Miyoshi

1+ million active installations   Tested with 4.8.4

Really Simple CAPTCHA

Really Simple CAPTCHA does not work alone and is intended to work with other plugins.

Captcha by BestWebSoft

1 super security anti-spam captcha plugin for WordPress forms.

SI CAPTCHA Anti-Spam

Adds Secure Image CAPTCHA on the forms for comments, login, registration, lost password, BuddyPress, bbPress, and more.

Google Captcha (reCAPTCHA) by BestWebSoft

Protect WordPress website forms from spam entries with Google reCaptcha.

Better WordPress reCAPTCHA (with no CAPTCHA reCAPTCHA)

This plugin utilizes Google reCAPTCHA to help your blog stay clear of spams. BWP reCAPTCHA

Invisible reCaptcha for WordPress

Invisible reCaptcha for WordPress plugin helps you to protect your sites against bad spam bots

Contact Plugins (22)

Contact Form 7

★★★★☆ (1,438)

Just another contact form plugin. Simple but flexible.

 Takayuki Miyoshi

 5+ million active installations Tested with 4.9.1

Contact Form 7

Just another contact form plugin. Simple but flexible.

Ninja Forms

Ninja Forms is the ultimate free form creation tool for WordPress. Build forms within minutes using a simple yet powerful drag-and-drop form creator.

Fast Secure Contact Form

An easy and powerful form builder that lets your visitors send you email.

Contact Widgets

Beautifully display social media and contact information on your website with these simple widgets.

Contact Form by BestWebSoft

Simple contact form plugin any WordPress website must have.

Simple Contact Form Plugin – PirateForms

Makes your contact form page more engaging by creating a good-looking simple WordPress contact form.

Flamingo

A trustworthy message storage plugin for Contact Form 7.

Contact Form 7 Honeypot

Contact Form 7 Honeypot – Adds honeypot anti-spam functionality to CF7 forms.

Visual Form Builder

Build beautiful, fully functional contact forms in only a few minutes without writing PHP, CSS, and more.

Contact Form 7 Datepicker

Easily add a date field using jQuery UI's date picker to your CF7 forms. This plugin.

Contact Form by WPForms – Drag & Drop Form Builder for WordPress

The best WordPress contact form plugin.

Contact Form by WD – responsive drag & drop contact form builder tool

Contact Form by WD plugin is a simple contact form builder tool, which allows the

Contact Form 7 Dynamic Text Extension

This plugin provides 2 new tag types for the Contact Form 7 Plugin.

MW WP Form

MW WP Form is shortcode base contact form plugin. This plugin have many feature. For

Contact Form Clean and Simple

A clean and simple AJAX contact form with Google reCAPTCHA, Twitter Bootstrap markup and Akismet

Contact Bank – Contact Forms Builder

Contact Bank is an ultimate form builder WordPress plugin that lets you create contact forms

Bootstrap for Contact Form 7

This plugin modifies the output of the popular Contact Form 7 plugin to be styled

Contact Form 7 Database Addon – CFDB7

Save and manage Contact Form 7 messages. Never lose important data. It is lightweight contact

Contact Form Clean and Simple

A clean and simple AJAX contact form with Google reCAPTCHA, Twitter Bootstrap markup and Akismet

Contact Form 7 Style

Simple style customization and templating for Contact Form 7 forms. Requires Contact Form 7 plugin

Conditional Fields for Contact Form 7

Adds conditional logic to Contact Form 7.

Contact Form 7 – Success Page Redirects

An add-on for Contact Form 7 that provides a straightforward method to redirect visitors to

Content Management Plugins (26)

Duplicate Post

★★★★★ (347)

Copy posts of any type with a click!

 Enrico Battocchi

2+ million active installations Tested with 4.9.1

Duplicate Post

Clone posts and pages.

Breadcrumb NavXT

Adds breadcrumb navigation showing the visitor's path to their current location.

Duplicate Page

Duplicate Posts, Pages and Custom Posts easily using single click.

WP Edit

Take complete control over the WordPress content editor.

Slideshow

Integrate a fancy slideshow in just five steps.

Table of Contents Plus

A powerful yet user friendly plugin that automatically creates a table of contents.

Title Remover

Gives you the ability to hide the title of any post, page or custom post.

Insert PHP

Run PHP code inserted into WordPress posts and pages.

List Category Posts

List Category Posts allows you to list posts by category in a post or page using the [catlist] shortcode.

Hide Title

Allows authors to hide the title on single pages and posts via the edit post.

WP Easy Columns

Easy Columns provides the shortcodes to create a grid system or magazine style columns.

Advanced Excerpt

Control the appearance of WordPress post excerpts.

Collapse-O-Matic

Collapse-O-Matic adds an [expand title="trigger text"]hidden content[/expand] shortcode that will wrap any content, including other.

Post Expirator

Allows you to add an expiration date to posts which you can configure to either.

Post Type Switcher

A simple way to change a post's type in WordPress

Page-list

[pagelist], [subpages], [siblings] and [pagelist_ext] shortcodes

Custom Post Template

Provides a drop-down to select different templates for posts from the post edit screen.

Page scroll to id

Create links that scroll the page smoothly to any id within the document.

Pods – Custom Content Types and Fields

Pods is a framework for creating, managing, and deploying customized content types and fields.

Dynamic "To Top" Plugin

Adds an automatic and dynamic "To Top" button to easily scroll long pages back to

Show Hide Author

Choose whether to show or hide the author's name.

Advanced iFrame

Include content the way YOU like in an iframe that can hide and modify elements

Tabby Responsive Tabs

Create responsive tabs inside your posts, pages or custom post content by adding simple shortcodes

WP Meta and Date Remover

Remove meta author and date information from posts and pages. Hide from Humans and Search

Real-Time Find and Replace

Set up find and replace rules that are executed AFTER a page is generated by

Public Post Preview

Enables you to give a link to anonymous users for public preview of a post

Comment & Spam Management Plugins (10)

Akismet Anti-Spam

★★★★★ (830)

Akismet checks your comments and contact form submissions against our global database of spam to...

 Automattic

 5+ million active installations Tested with 4.9.1

Akismet

Akismet checks your comments and contact form submissions against our global database of spam to prevent your site from publishing malicious content.

Disable Comments

Allows administrators to globally disable comments on their site.

Antispam Bee

Easy and extremely productive spam-fighting plugin with many sophisticated solutions.

Anti-spam

No spam in comments. No captcha.

Facebook Comments

Facebook comments can be annoying to set up. This plugin makes it simple to add the Facebook comments system to your WordPress site without any hassle.

Spam FireWall, Anti-Spam by CleanTalk

Spam protection, anti-spam, all-in-one, premium plug-in. No spam comments & users, no spam contact.

No Page Comment

An admin interface to control the default comment and trackback settings on new posts, pages

Stop Spammers

Aggressive anti-spam plugin that eliminates comment spam, trackback spam, contact form spam and registration spam.

WP-SpamShield Anti-Spam – All-in-One Spam Protection

All-in-one WordPress spam protection, with NO CAPTCHAs, challenge questions or other inconvenience to site visitors.

Comments – wpDiscuz

AJAX powered realtime comments. Designed to extend WordPress native comments. Custom comment forms and fields

Communication Plugins (4)

Zendesk Chat

Zendesk Chat (previously Zopim) lets you monitor and chat with visitors surfing your store.

Tawk.to Live Chat

(OFFICIAL tawk.to plugin) Instantly chat with visitors on your website with the free tawk.to chat.

Call Now Button

A very simple yet very effective plugin that adds a Call Now button to your site.

WP Live Chat Support

Fully functional Live Chat plugin. Chat with your visitors for free! No need for monthly

Community & Membership Plugins (8)

bbPress

bbPress is forum software, made the WordPress way.

BuddyPress

BuddyPress helps site builders and WordPress developers add community features to their websites.

Members

The most powerful user, role, and capability management plugin for WordPress.

WP-Members: Membership Framework

WP-Members™ is a free membership management framework for WordPress® that restricts content to registered users.

Subscribe to Comments

Subscribe to Comments allows commenters on an entry to subscribe to e-mail notifications for subsequent.

Paid Memberships Pro

A revenue-generating machine for membership sites. Unlimited levels with recurring payment, protected content and member.

Ultimate Member

The easiest way to create powerful online communities and beautiful user profiles with WordPress

s2Member Framework (Member Roles, Capabilities, Membership, PayPal Members)

s2Member®—a powerful (free) membership plugin for WordPress®. Protect members only content with roles/capabilities.

E-Commerce & WooCommerce Plugins (30)

WooCommerce

⭐⭐⭐⭐ (2,661)

WooCommerce is a powerful, extendable eCommerce plugin that helps you sell anything. Beautifully.

 Automattic

 3+ million active installations Tested with 4.9.1

WooCommerce

WooCommerce is a powerful, extendable eCommerce plugin that helps you sell anything. Beautifully.

YITH WooCommerce Wishlist

YITH WooCommerce Wishlist add all Wishlist features to your website. Needs

WooCommerce to work.

WooCommerce Stripe Payment Gateway

Take credit card payments on your store using Stripe.

YITH WooCommerce Compare

YITH WooCommerce Compare allows you to compare more products of your shop in one complete.

YITH WooCommerce Zoom Magnifier

YITH WooCommerce Zoom Magnifier add zoom effect to product images and a customizable image slider.

YITH WooCommerce Ajax Product Filter

WooCommerce Ajax Product Filter lets you apply the filters you need to display the correct WooCommerce variations of the products you are looking for.

WordPress Download Manager

This File Management & Digital Store plugin which will help you to control file downloads

WooCommerce PDF Invoices & Packing Slips

Create, print & automatically email PDF invoices & packing slips for WooCommerce orders.

Easy Digital Downloads

The easiest way to sell digital products with WordPress.

WooCommerce Multilingual – run WooCommerce with WPML

Allows running fully multilingual e-commerce sites using WooCommerce and WPML.

YITH WooCommerce Quick View

This plugin adds the possibility to have a quick preview of the products right from

WooCommerce Grid / List toggle

Adds a grid/list view toggle to product archives

WooCommerce Customizer

Helps you customize WooCommerce without writing any code!

WooCommerce Menu Cart

Automatically displays a shopping cart in your menu bar. Works with WooCommerce,

WP-Ecommerce, EDD, Eshop

WooCommerce Print Invoice & Delivery Note

Print invoices and delivery notes for WooCommerce orders.

Persian Woocommerce

This plugin extends the WooCommerce shop plugin with complete Persian(Farsi) language packs

WooCommerce PagSeguro

Adds PagSeguro gateway to the WooCommerce plugin

Saphali Woocommerce Russian

Набор русских дополнений к интернет-магазину на Woocommerce. Adds Russian localization & special Tools in WooCommerce.

Woocommerce CSV importer

Import products into woocommerce.

Booster for WooCommerce

Supercharge your WordPress WooCommerce site with these awesome powerful features.

WooCommerce Checkout Field Editor (Manager) Pro

WooCommerce Checkout Field Editor Pro – The best WooCommerce checkout manager plugin to customize checkout

WooCommerce Products Filter

WooCommerce Products Filter – flexible, easy and robust professional filter for products in the WooCommerce

WordPress Simple PayPal Shopping Cart

Very easy to use Simple WordPress PayPal Shopping Cart Plugin. Great for selling products online

WooCommerce Print Invoice & Delivery Notes

Print invoices and delivery notes for WooCommerce orders.

Custom Product Tabs for WooCommerce

Add custom tabs with content to products in WooCommerce.

WooCommerce Cart Tab

Adds an offscreen cart to all pages on your site and a fixed tab that

PayPal for WooCommerce

Upgrade your WooCommerce PayPal experience for free! Developed by an Ace Certified PayPal Developer, Official

WooCommerce Germanized

Extends WooCommerce to become a legally compliant Shop for German Market. Must Have for every

WooCommerce Correios

Integration between the Correios and WooCommerce

Product Import Export for WooCommerce

Easily import products into WooCommerce store or export WooCommerce products from the store. Import WooCommerce

E-Mail & SMTP Plugins (17)

WP Mail SMTP

The most popular SMTP plugin on WordPress.org. Trusted by over 600k sites.

MailPoet Newsletters

Send newsletters post notifications or autoresponders from WordPress easily, and beautifully.

Newsletter

Add a real newsletter system to your blog. For free. With unlimited newsletters and subscribers.

Easy WP SMTP

Easily send emails from your WordPress blog using your preferred SMTP server

Postman SMTP Mailer/Email Log

Postman is a next-generation SMTP Mailer, software that assists in the delivery of email generated content.

Genesis eNews Extended

Creates a new widget to easily add mailing lists integration to a Genesis website.

Email Address Encoder

A lightweight plugin to protect email addresses from email-harvesting robots by encoding them into decimal.

WP SMTP

WP SMTP can help us to send emails via SMTP instead of the PHP mail().

Configure SMTP

Configure SMTP mailing in WordPress, including support for sending e-mail via

SSL/TLS (such as GMail).

SendGrid

Send emails and upload contacts through SendGrid from your WordPress installation using SMTP or API.

Contact Form 7 MailChimp Extension

Simple way to integrate MailChimp mailing lists to Contact Form 7. Save your subscribers in

Mail Bank – PHP Mail & SMTP Plugin

Mail Bank reconfigures the Mail Function and provides sophisticated SMTP settings to send and log

WP Subscribe

WP Subscribe is a simple but powerful subscription plugin which supports MailChimp, Aweber and Feedburner.

wpMandrill

The wpMandrill plugin sends emails that are generated by WordPress through Mandrill, a transactional email

Newsletter Sign-Up

Integrate your WordPress site with 3rd-party newsletter services like Aweber and YMLP. Adds various sign-up

Check Email

Check email allows you to test if your WordPress installation is sending emails correctly by

SMTP Mailer

Configure a SMTP server to send email from your WordPress site. Configure the wp_mail() function

Form Builder & Popups Plugins (23)

Ninja Forms – The Easy and Powerful Forms Builder

 ⭐⭐⭐⭐½ (845)

Drag and drop fields in an intuitive UI to create contact forms, email subscription forms,...

 The WP Ninjas

 1+ million active installations ⓦ Tested with 4.8.4

Ninja Forms

Ninja Forms is the ultimate free form creation tool for WordPress. Build forms within minutes using a simple yet powerful drag-and-drop form creator.

OptinMonster – Best WordPress Popup and Lead Generation Plugin

OptinMonster helps you grow your email list by converting visitors into subscribers and customers.

MailChimp for WordPress

MailChimp for WordPress helps you add more subscribers to your MailChimp lists using various methods.

Free Tools to Automate Your Site Growth

Free and easy way to double your email subscribers, plus sharing tools to double your traffic.

Email Subscribers & Newsletters

Add subscription forms on website, send HTML newsletters & automatically notify subscribers about new blog.

MailChimp Forms by MailMunch

MailChimp Forms to get more email subscribers.

Easy Forms for MailChimp

The ultimate MailChimp WordPress plugin. Easily build unlimited forms for your

MailChimp lists, add them.

Formidable Forms

The best WordPress form plugin.

amoForms

Create forms and manage submissions easily with a simple interface.

Form Maker by WD – user-friendly drag & drop Form Builder plugin

Form Maker is a fresh and innovative form builder.

Form Builder

Form Builder is an intuitive tool for creating contact forms rearranging and editing fields.

Hustle – Pop-Ups, Slide-ins and Email Opt-ins

The complete marketing plugin for email opt-ins, pop-up advertising and building your user base.

Caldera Forms – More Than Contact Forms

Responsive form builder for contact forms, user registration and login forms, Mailchimp, and more.

Web-Settler Forms – Create Responsive Contact Forms

Contact form saves your hours of precious time by making contact form creation process super

Popup

Popup Builder is the most complete pop up plugin. Html, image, shortcode and many other

Popups – WordPress Popup

Most complete free Popups plugin, scroll triggered popups, compatible with social networks, Gravity Forms, Ninja

Forms – Form builder and Contact form

Form builder are one of the most important elements of your website. If you need

Popups, Welcome Bar, Optins and Lead Generation Plugin – Icegram

Grow your subscriber list, engage and convert visitors, decrease bounce rate with this best in

Easy Modal

The #1 WordPress Popup Plugin! Make glorious & powerful popups and market your content like

Popup Maker

Create any popup imaginable! Customize your popups from head-to-toe and give your site more utility.

HubSpot – Free Marketing Plugin for WordPress

Add the free HubSpot Marketing plugin to your WordPress site! Easy to set up.

Popup by Supsystic

Popup by Supsystic is the best way to convert visitors into subscribers, followers & customers

Form Builder | Create Responsive Contact Forms

Form builder is a user friendly drag & drop plugin. This Form Builder will let

Favicon (3)

All In One Favicon

Easily add a Favicon to your site and the WordPress admin pages.

Favicon by RealFaviconGenerator

Generate and setup a favicon for desktop browsers, iPhone/iPad, Android devices, Windows 8 tablets, and more.

Favicon Rotator

Easily set site favicon and even rotate through multiple icons

Font Plugins (7)

Easy Google Fonts

Adds google fonts to any theme without coding and integrates with the WordPress Customizer automatically.

WP Google Fonts

The WP Google Fonts plugin allows you to easily add fonts from the Google Font palette.

Use Any Font

Embed any font in your website.

Disable Google Fonts

Disable enqueuing of Open Sans and other fonts used by WordPress from Google.

Font – official webfonts plugin of Fonts For Web. NO CODING! Just click & change font size, color and font face visually!

Finally official* web fonts plugin for WordPress. CLICK ON ANYTHING TO CHANGE IT(see screenshots)! Then

WP SVG Icons

Quickly and effortlessly enable 490+ beautifully designed SVG font icons, available on the frontend and

Styles

Be creative with colors and fonts. Styles changes everything.

Google Related Plugins (5)

Google Doc Embedder

Let's you embed PDF, MS Office, and many other file types in a web page.

Use Google Libraries

Allows your site to use common JavaScript libraries from Google's AJAX Libraries CDN.

DuracellTomi's Google Tag Manager for WordPress

The first Google Tag Manager plugin for WordPress with business goals in mind.

Verify Google Webmaster Tools

Adds Google Webmaster Tools verification meta tag and gets account verified.

Google Authenticator

Google Authenticator for your WordPress blog.

Image & Media Plugins (56)

Regenerate Thumbnails

★★★★½ (293)

Allows you to regenerate your thumbnails after changing the thumbnail sizes.

 Alex Mills (Viper007Bond)

1+ million active installations Tested with 4.9.1

Regenerate Thumbnails

Allows you to regenerate your thumbnails after changing the thumbnail sizes.

Force Regenerate Thumbnails

Delete and REALLY force the regenerate thumbnail.

Image Widget

Image Widget is a simple plugin that uses the native WordPress media manager to add image widgets to your site.

EWWW Image Optimizer

Reduce image sizes in WordPress including NextGEN, GRAND FlAGallery, FooGallery and more using lossless/lossy methods.

Photo Gallery by WD – Responsive Photo Gallery for WordPress

Photo Gallery is an advanced plugin with a list of tools and options for adding photos.

Easy FancyBox

Easily enable the FancyBox jQuery extension on just about all media links.

Responsive Lightbox by dFactory

Responsive Lightbox allows users to view larger versions of images and galleries in a lightbox.

Enable Media Replace

This plugin allows you to replace a file in your media library by uploading a new file in its place.

Imsanity

Imsanity automatically resizes huge image uploads.

Simple Lightbox

The highly customizable lightbox for WordPress.

Auto Post Thumbnail

Automatically generate the Post Thumbnail (Featured Thumbnail) from the first image in post.

WP Lightbox 2

WP Lightbox 2 is awesome tool for adding responsive lightbox effect for images.

iframe

Speedup and protect WordPress in a smart way.

Video Thumbnails

Video Thumbnails simplifies the process of automatically displaying video thumbnails in your WordPress template.

AJAX Thumbnail Rebuild

AJAX Thumbnail Rebuild allows you to rebuild all thumbnails at once without script timeouts on your site.

FancyBox for WordPress

Seamlessly integrates FancyBox into your blog: Upload, activate, and you're done. Additional configuration optional.

Enhanced Media Library

A better management for WordPress Media Library.

WP jQuery Lightbox

A drop-in replacement for Lightbox 2 and similar plugins.

Gallery – Photo Gallery

Gallery image is the best gallery plugin to use if you want to be original.

Add From Server

"Add From Server" is a quick plugin which allows you to import media & files.

Simple Image Sizes

This plugin allow create custom image sizes for your site. Override your theme sizes directly.

Gallery by Envira – Responsive Photo Gallery for WordPress

The best WordPress gallery plugin. Drag & Drop photo gallery builder that helps you create.

Foo Gallery

Foo Gallery is the most intuitive and extensible gallery management tool ever created for WordPress.

WordPress Button Plugin MaxButtons

WordPress button plugin so powerful and easy to use anyone can create beautiful buttons and.

SVG Support

Allow SVG file uploads using the WordPress Media Library uploader plus direct styling/animation of SVG.

Dynamic Featured Image

Dynamically adds multiple featured image (post thumbnail) functionality to posts, pages and custom post types.

jQuery Colorbox

Adds Colorbox/Lightbox functionality to images, grouped by post or page. Works for

Get the Image

An easy-to-use image script for adding things such as thumbnail, slider, gallery, and feature images.

Lightbox

Lightbox is the perfect tool for viewing photos.

Multiple Post Thumbnails

Adds multiple post thumbnails to a post type. If you've ever wanted more than one.

Photo Gallery by Supsystic

Photo Gallery with visual editor to build amazing photo gallery.

Advanced Responsive Video Embedder

Easy responsive video embeds via URLs or shortcodes. Perfect drop-in replacement for WordPress' default embeds.

Better Font Awesome

The Better Font Awesome plugin for WordPress. Shortcodes, HTML, TinyMCE, various Font Awesome versions, backwards.

WP Gallery Custom Links

Specify custom links for WordPress gallery images (instead of attachment or file only).

Gallery – Portfolio Gallery

Gallery – Portfolio Gallery is a great plugin for adding specialized portfolio galleriey, video portfolio.

Post Thumbnail Editor

Fed up with the lack of automated tools to properly crop and scale post thumbnails?

Imagify Image Optimizer

Dramatically reduce image file sizes without losing quality, make your website load faster, boost your.

Resize Image After Upload

Behind-the-scenes plugin to automatically resize images when uploaded, restricting size to within specified maximum h/w.

Menu Image

Adds a field to load the image in a menu item and displays the image

WP Photo Album Plus

This plugin is designed to easily manage and display your photos, photo albums, slideshows and

Media Library Assistant

Enhances the Media Library; powerful [mla_gallery] [mla_tag_cloud] [mla_term_list], taxonomy support, IPTC/EXIF/XMP/PDF processing, bulk/quick edit.

Slideshow Gallery

Feature content in a JavaScript powered slideshow gallery showcase on your WordPress website

Ultimate Responsive Image Slider

Add Fully Responsive Image Slider To Your WordPress Blog

Responsive Photo Gallery for WordPress by Gallery Bank

Gallery Bank is an advanced plugin which creates Beautiful Photo Galleries and Albums for different

Gallery – Flagallery Photo Portfolio

Gallery Portfolio, Photo Gallery, Video Gallery, Music Album & Banner Rotator plugin with powerfull admin

Video Embed & Thumbnail Generator

Makes video thumbnails, allows resolution switching, and embeds responsive self-hosted videos and galleries.

Image Watermark

Image Watermark allows you to automatically watermark images uploaded to the WordPress Media Library and

Easy Watermark

Allows to add watermark to images automatically on upload or manually.

Optimus – WordPress Image Optimizer

Effective image compression and optimization during the upload process. Smart, automatic and reliable.

Tiled Gallery Carousel Without JetPack

Tiled Gallery Carousel allows you to display image galleries in mosaic styles without Jetpack.

Gallery – Photo Gallery and Images Gallery

Gallery modes photo gallery, images gallery, video gallery, Polaroid gallery, gallery lighbox, portfolio gallery, responsive

Attachments

Attachments allows you to simply append any number of items from your WordPress Media Library

Manual Image Crop

Plugin allows you to manually crop all the image sizes registered in your WordPress theme

WP Featherlight – A Simple jQuery Lightbox

An ultra-lightweight jQuery lightbox for WordPress images and galleries.

Pixabay Images

Find quality CC0 Public Domain images for commercial use, and add them to your blog

Kraken.io Image Optimizer

Requires at least: 3.0.1 Tested up to: 4.7.4 Donate link: https://kraken.io Stable tag: 2.6.2

Language & Translation Plugins (9)

Loco Translate

Translate WordPress plugins and themes directly in your browser.

Polylang

Making WordPress multilingual.

Rus-To-Lat

Converts Cyrillic characters in post slugs to Latin characters.

qTranslate X

Adds a user-friendly multilingual dynamic content management.

Cyr to Lat enhanced

Converts Cyrillic, European and Georgian characters in post, page and term slugs to Latin characters.

Google Language Translator

Welcome to Google Language Translator! This plugin allows you to insert the Google Language Translator.

Translate WordPress with GTranslate

Translate WordPress with Google Translate multilanguage plugin to make your website multilingual.

Crayon Syntax Highlighter

Syntax Highlighter supporting multiple languages, themes, fonts, highlighting from a URL, or post text.

WPML Widgets

WPML Widgets is a simple to use extension to add a language selector dropdown to

Font Awesome 4 Menus

Allows you to add Font Awesome 4 icons to your WordPress menus or anywhere on

Login Plugins (12)

Nextend Facebook Connect

One click registration & login plugin for Facebook? Easy installation? Is it totally free.

Login With Ajax

Add smooth ajax login/registration effects and choose where users get redirected upon log in/out.

Sidebar Login

Easily add an ajax-enhanced login widget to your WordPress site sidebar.

WordPress Social Login

WordPress Social Login allow your visitors to comment and login with social networks such as.

Uber Login Logo

A simple, lightweight WordPress plugin to change your login logo.

Nextend Google Connect

One click registration & login plugin for Google? Easy installation? Is it totally free and

Theme My Login

Themes the WordPress login pages according to your theme.

Social Login

Allow your visitors to comment and login with social networks like Twitter, Facebook, Paypal, LinkedIn,

Login Logo

Customize the logo on the WP login screen by simply dropping a file named login-logo.png.

Erident Custom Login and Dashboard

Customize completely your WordPress Login Screen easily. Add your logo, change background image, colors, styles

Add Logo to Admin

Add a custom logo to your wp-admin and login page.

Customize WordPress Login Page

Customize Your WordPress Login Screen Amazingly – Add Own Logo, Add Social Profiles, Login Form

Map Plugins (14)

WP Google Maps

The easiest to use Google maps plugin!

MapPress Easy Google Maps

MapPress is the most popular and easiest way to create great-looking Google Maps.

Google Maps Widget

Tired of buggy and slow Google Maps plugins taking hours to setup?

Comprehensive Google Map Plugin

A simple and intuitive, yet elegant and fully documented Google map plugin that installs as.

WP Google Map Plugin

A Google Maps plugin for WordPress to create unlimited locations, maps and display google map.

Google Maps – Google Maps Builder for WordPress

Google Map plugin form Huge-IT-the best solution to add awesome Google Maps to your website.

API KEY for Google Maps

Retroactively add Google Maps API KEY to any theme or plugin.

WordPress Google Maps Plugin

A simple, easy and quite powerful Google Maps tool to create, manage and embed custom

Leaflet Maps Marker (Google Maps, OpenStreetMap, Bing Maps)

The most comprehensive & user-friendly mapping solution for WordPress

Simple Map

Easy way to embed google map(s).

Visitor Maps and Who's Online

Displays Visitor Maps with location pins, city, and country. Includes a Who's Online Sidebar. Has

Google Maps Easy

WordPress Google Maps

Maps Builder – Google Maps Plugin

The most flexible, robust, and easy to use WordPress plugin for creating powerful Google Maps

WP Store Locator

An easy to use location management system that enables users to search for nearby physical

Miscellaneous (30)

WP Multibyte Patch

Multibyte functionality enhancement for the WordPress Japanese package.

WP Job Manager

Manage job listings from the WordPress admin panel, and allow users to post job listings

Download Monitor

Download Monitor is a plugin for uploading and managing downloads, tracking downloads, and displaying links.

PDF Embedder

Embed PDFs straight into your posts and pages, with intelligent resizing of width and height.

Really Simple CSV Importer

Alternative CSV Importer plugin. Simple and powerful, best for geeks.

Import any XML or CSV File to WordPress

WP All Import is an extremely powerful importer that makes it easy to import any.

FeedWordPress

FeedWordPress syndicates content from feeds you choose into your WordPress weblog.

One Click Demo Import

Import your demo content, widgets and theme settings with one click. Theme authors! Enable simple demo import for your theme demo data.

Heartbeat Control

Allows you to easily manage the frequency of the WordPress heartbeat API.

PowerPress Podcasting plugin by Blubrry

No. 1 Podcasting plugin for WordPress, with simple & advanced modes, players, subscribe tools, and.

Disable Emojis

This plugin disables the new WordPress emoji functionality.

WP Total Hacks

WP Total Hacks can customize more than 20 settings on your WordPress Site. PHP5 is

Easy Smooth Scroll Links

Create anchors and add up to to 30 scrolling animation effects to links that link

SoundCloud Shortcode

SoundCloud Shortcode plugin for WordPress

No Self Pings

Keeps WordPress from sending pings to your own site.

Compact WP Audio Player

A Compact WP Audio Player Pluign that is compatible with all major browsers and devices

WP RSS Aggregator

WP RSS Aggregator is the most comprehensive RSS feed importer and autoblogging plugin for WordPress

Multi Device Switcher

This WordPress plugin allows you to set a separate theme for device (Smart Phone, Tablet

WP-Print

Displays a printable version of your WordPress blog's post/page.

Logo Carousel

Show your partners, clients or sponsors on your website in a logo carousel!

Ditty News Ticker

Ditty News Ticker is a multi-functional data display plugin.

Gwolle Guestbook

Gwolle Guestbook is the WordPress guestbook you've just been looking for. Beautiful and easy.

Embed Any Document

Easiest way to upload and display PDF, MS Office and more documents on your WordPress

MP3-jPlayer

Easy, Flexible Audio for WordPress.

MediaElement.js – HTML5 Video & Audio Player

MediaElement.js is an HTML5 video and audio player with Flash fallback and captions. Supports IE

WordPress Ping Optimizer

Save your WordPress blog from getting tagged as ping spammer.

OneSignal – Free Web Push Notifications

Increase engagement and drive more repeat traffic to your WordPress site with desktop push notifications

Give – Donation Plugin and Fundraising Platform

Accept donations and begin fundraising with Give, the highest rated WordPress donation plugin for online

WP Offload S3 Lite

Copies files to Amazon S3 as they are uploaded to the Media Library. Optionally configure

WordPress Charts and Graphs Lite

A simple and quite powerful WordPress chart plugin to create and embed interactive charts &

Online Course Management (1)

LearnPress – WordPress LMS Plugin

A WordPress LMS Plugin to create WordPress Learning Management System. Turn your WP to LMS

Poll, Rating, Survey, and Testimonial Plugins (9)

WP-Polls

Adds an AJAX poll system to your WordPress blog.

WP-PostRatings

Adds an AJAX rating system for your WordPress site's content.

WP Product Review Lite

Easily turn your basic posts into in-depth reviews with ratings, pros and cons, affiliate links.

WP Customer Reviews

Allows your visitors to leave business / product reviews.

Testimonials Widget

Easily add social proofing to your website with Testimonials Widget. List or slide reviews via.

kk Star Ratings

kk Star Ratings allows blog visitors to involve and interact more effectively with your website

Testimonials Plugin: Easy Testimonials

Testimonials widget and shortcode for adding Testimonials to your WordPress Theme, with a simple interface.

Testimonial Rotator

Easily add Testimonials to your WordPress Blog or Company Website.

Strong Testimonials

Simple yet powerful. Very customizable. Developer-friendly. Free support.

Popular, Recent, & Related Post Plugins (11)

WordPress Popular Posts

A highly customizable, easy-to-use popular posts widget!

Yet Another Related Posts Plugin (YARPP)

Display a list of related posts on your site based on a powerful unique algorithm.

Recent Posts Widget Extended

Provides flexible and advanced recent posts.

WordPress Related Posts

WordPress Related Posts – the plugin for related posts with thumbnails. Caching included.

Recent Posts Widget With Thumbnails

List of your site's most recent posts, with clickable title and thumbnails.

Contextual Related Posts

Display related posts on your WordPress blog and feed. Supports thumbnails, shortcodes, widgets and custom.

Similar Posts – Powerful Related Posts Plugin

Displays a list of related posts similar to the current one based on content, title.

Related Posts

Link to related content to help your readers. Get attention from other authors. Make great

Related Posts

Related posts a so easy and fast

Top 10 – Popular posts plugin for WordPress

Track daily and total visits on your blog posts. Display the count as well as

Related Posts

Related Posts is The Best Customizable plugin, that nicely displays related posts thumbnails under the

Redirection & Link Management Plugins (24)

Broken Link Checker

★★★★☆ (339)

This plugin will check your posts, comments and other content for broken links and missing...

Janis Elsts, Vladimir Prelovac

500,000+ active installations   Tested with 4.8.4

Broken Link Checker

This plugin will check your posts, comments and other content for broken links and missing links.

Redirection

Redirection is a WordPress plugin to manage 301 redirections and keep track of 404 errors.

Page Links To

This plugin allows you to make a WordPress page or post link to a URL of your choosing, instead of its WordPress page or post URL.

Quick Page/Post Redirect Plugin

Easily redirect pages/posts or custom post types to another page/post or external URL.

Simple 301 Redirects

Simple 301 Redirects provides an easy method of redirecting requests to another page on your site.

Pretty Link Lite

Shrink, beautify, track, manage and share any URL on or off your WordPress website.

Link Manager

Enables the Link Manager that existed in WordPress until version 3.5.

Velvet Blues Update URLs

Updates all URLs and content links in your website.

All 404 Redirect to Homepage

By using this smart plugin, you can fix all 404-error links by redirecting them.

Custom Permalinks

Set custom permalinks on a per-post, per-tag or per-category basis.

404 to 301

Automatically redirect, log and notify all 404 page errors to any page using 301 redirect.

Custom Post Type Permalinks

Edit the permalink of custom post type.

No Category Base (WPML)

This plugin removes the mandatory 'Category Base' from your category permalinks.

.html on PAGES

Appends .html to the URL of PAGES when using permalinks.

404 Redirection

Permanently redirect all 404's to the main blog URL. The primary purpose is to salvage.

404 to Start

Send 404 page not found error directly to start page (or any other page/site) to.

SEO Redirection Plugin

SEO Redirection is the best plugin to manage 301 redirections without requiring knowledge of Apache

Eggplant 301 Redirects

Easily manage and create 301 redirects for your WordPress website.

Remove Category URL

This plugin removes '/category' from your category permalinks. (e.g. /category/my-category/ to /my-category/)

Safe Redirect Manager

Safely and easily manage your website's HTTP redirects.

Open external links in a new window

Opens all (or specific) external links in a new window. XHTML Strict compliant and search

External Links

The external links plugin for WordPress lets you process outgoing links differently from internal links.

404page – your smart custom 404 error page

Custom 404 the easy way! Set any page as custom 404 error page. No coding

Go Live Update URLS

Goes through entire site and replaces all instances of and old url with a new

Security Plugins (37)

Jetpack by WordPress.com

Keep any WordPress site secure, increase traffic, and engage your readers.

Limit Login Attempts Reloaded

Reloaded version of the original Limit Login Attempts plugin for Login Protection by a team

Wordfence Security

⭐⭐⭐⭐⭐ (3,160)

Secure your website with the most comprehensive WordPress security plugin. Firewall, malware scan, blocking, live...

 Wordfence

 2+ million active installations Ⓦ Tested with 4.9.1

Wordfence Security

Secure your website with the most comprehensive WordPress security plugin.

iThemes Security (formerly Better WP Security)

iThemes Security is the #1 WordPress Security Plugin.

All in One WP Security & Firewall

A comprehensive, user-friendly, all in one WordPress security and firewall plugin for your site.

Loginizer

Loginizer is a WordPress security plugin which helps you fight against bruteforce attacks.

Sucuri Security – Auditing, Malware Scanner and Security Hardening

The Sucuri WordPress Security plugin is a toolset for security integrity monitoring, malware detection, and more.

MainWP Child

Provides a secure connection between your MainWP Dashboard and your WordPress sites.

Login LockDown

Limits the number of login attempts from a given IP range within a certain time.

Anti-Malware Security and Brute-Force Firewall

This Anti-Malware scanner searches for Malware, Viruses, and other security threats and vulnerabilities on your website.

Really Simple SSL

No setup required! You only need an SSL certificate, and this plugin will do the rest.

Rename wp-login.php

Change wp-login.php to anything you want.

Password Protected

A very simple way to quickly password protect your WordPress site with a single password.

WPS Hide Login

Change wp-login.php to anything you want.

BulletProof Security

Secure WordPress Website Security Protection: Firewall Security, Login Security, Database Security & Backup.

AntiVirus

Security plugin to protect your blog or website against exploits and spam injections.

WordPress HTTPS (SSL)

WordPress HTTPS is intended to be an all-in-one solution to using SSL on WordPress sites.

Theme Authenticity Checker

Scan all of your theme files for potentially malicious or unwanted code.

SSL Insecure Content Fixer

Clean up WordPress website HTTPS insecure content.

Peter's Login Redirect

Redirect users to different locations after logging in and logging out.

BBQ: Block Bad Queries

The fastest firewall plugin for WordPress.

Custom Login Page Customizer

Custom Login Customizer allows you to easily customize your admin login page, straight from your.

Acunetix Secure WordPress

plugins, private, protection, tracking, WordPress Requires at least: 3.0 Tested up to: 4.2 Stable tag

Timthumb Vulnerability Scanner

Scans your wp-content directory for vulnerable instances of timthumb.php, and optionally upgrades them to a.

WP Content Copy Protection & No Right Click

This wp plugin protect the posts content from being copied by any other web site.

Shield Security

Protect your website, your reputation, and your customers for free with Shield Security, the most.

WP Security Audit Log

Keep an audit trail of all changes and under the hood WordPress activity to ensure

WP-CopyProtect [Protect your blog posts]

Protect your blog content from getting copied. A simple plug-in developed to stop the Copy

Login Logout Menu

You can now add a correct login & logout link in your WP menus.

VaultPress

VaultPress is a subscription service offering real-time backup, automated security scanning, and support from WordPress

WP Content Copy Protection

WP Content Copy Protection uses aggressive techniques in protecting your online content (text/source/images/video/audio) from being

CloudFlare Flexible SSL

Fix For CloudFlare Flexible SSL Redirect Loop For WordPress.

WP Limit Login Attempts

Limit Login Attempts for login protection. Limit rate of login attempts and block IP temporarily.

BruteProtect

BruteProtect is no longer actively supported. All new development is now being done on the

WP fail2ban

Write a myriad of WordPress events to syslog for integration with fail2ban.

WP Force SSL

This plugin helps you redirect HTTP traffic to HTTPS without the need of touching any

Hide My Site

Choose a single password to protect your entire wordpress site from the public and search

SEO & Search Plugins (16)

Yoast SEO

★★★★★ (17,397)

Improve your WordPress SEO: Write better content and have a fully optimized WordPress site using...

 Team Yoast

 5+ million active installations Tested with 4.9.1

Yoast SEO

WordPress out of the box is already technically quite a good platform for SEO.

All in One SEO Pack

The original SEO plugin for WordPress, downloaded over 30,000,000 times since 2007.

Meta Slider

The most popular WordPress slider plugin. Creating slideshows with Meta Slider is fast and easy. Simply select images from your WordPress Media Library, drag and drop them into place, set slide captions, links and SEO fields all from one page.

SEO Ultimate

This all-in-one SEO plugin gives you control over meta titles & descriptions, open graph, auto-linking, and more.

Add Meta Tags

A metadata plugin that can optimize your web site for more efficient indexing and easier.

Search & Replace

Search & Replace data in your database with WordPress admin, replace domains/URLs of your WordPress.

Relevanssi – A Better Search

Relevanssi replaces the default search with a partial-match search that sorts results by relevance.

Search Everything

Search Everything increases WordPress' default search functionality in three easy steps.

Search Regex

Search Regex adds a powerful set of search and replace functions to WordPress that go.

All In One Schema.org Rich Snippets

Boost CTR. Improve SEO & Rankings. Supports most of the content type. Works perfectly with.

Facebook Open Graph, Google+ and Twitter Card Tags

Inserts Facebook Open Graph, Google+/Schema.org, Twitter and SEO Meta Tags into your WordPress Website for.

SEO by SQUIRRLY™

SEO Plugin By Squirrly is for the NON-SEO experts. Get Excellent SEO with Better Content,

WP External Links (nofollow new tab seo)

Open external links in a new tab / window, add "nofollow", "noopener" and font icons,

Glue for Yoast SEO & AMP

This plugin makes sure the default WordPress AMP plugin uses the proper Yoast SEO metadata

Better Search Replace

A simple plugin to update URLs or other text in a database.

The SEO Framework

The SEO Framework plugin provides an automated and advanced SEO solution for your WordPress website.

Shortcode & Code Plugins (10)

Shortcodes Ultimate

★★★★★ (4,341)

A comprehensive collection of visual components for your site

 Vladimir Anokhin

 700,000+ active installations Tested with 4.9.1

Shortcodes Ultimate

Supercharge your WordPress theme with mega pack of shortcodes.

Display Posts Shortcode

Display a listing of posts using the [display-posts] shortcode.

Easy Bootstrap Shortcode

Easy Bootstrap Shortcode enable you to add bootstrap 3.0.3 styles in your pages, post and

Bootstrap Shortcodes for WordPress

Implements Bootstrap 3 styles and components in WordPress through shortcodes.

Posts in Page

Easily add one or more posts to any page using simple shortcodes.

Code Snippets

An easy, clean and simple way to add code snippets to your site.

Shortcodes by Angie Makes

A plugin that adds a useful family of shortcodes to your WordPress theme.

Column Shortcodes

Adds shortcodes to easily create columns in your posts or pages.

Raw HTML

Lets you use raw HTML or any other code in your posts. You can also

Shortcoder

Create custom "Shortcodes" easily for HTML, JavaScript snippets and use the shortcodes within posts, pages

Site Administration Plugins (95)

Advanced Custom Fields

★★★★★ (989)

Customise WordPress with powerful, professional and intuitive fields.

  Elliot Condon

1+ million active installations Tested with 4.9.0

Advanced Custom Fields

Customize WordPress with powerful, professional and intuitive fields.

WP-PageNavi

Adds a more advanced paging navigation interface.

WP-Optimize

WP-Optimize is an effective tool for automatically cleaning your WordPress database so that it runs at maximum efficiency.

Post Types Order

A powerful plugin, Order Posts and Post Types Objects using a Drag and Drop Sortable JavaScript capability.

Custom Post Type UI

Admin UI for creating custom post types and custom taxonomies for WordPress.

InfiniteWP Client

Install this plugin on unlimited sites and manage them all from a central dashboard.

ManageWP Worker

ManageWP is the ultimate WordPress productivity tool, allowing you to efficiently manage your websites.

All-in-One WP Migration

All-in-One WP Migration is the only tool that you will ever need to migrate a website.

WP Clone by WP Academy

Move or copy a WordPress site to another server or to another domain name, move, and more.

Simple Page Ordering

Order your pages and other hierarchical post types with simple drag and drop.

Toolset Types

The complete and reliable plugin for managing custom post types, custom taxonomies and custom fields.

Category Order and Taxonomy Terms Order

Order Categories and all custom taxonomies terms (hierarchically) and child terms using a drag and drop.

Meta Box

Meta Box plugin is a powerful, professional developer toolkit to create custom meta boxes.

Exclude Pages

This plugin adds a checkbox, "include this page in menus", uncheck this to exclude pages.

WP Migrate DB

Migrates your database by running find & replace on URLs and file paths, handling serialized.

Admin Menu Editor

Let's you edit the WordPress admin menu.

Insert Headers and Footers

This plugin allows you to add extra scripts to the header and footer of your site.

Adminimize

Adminimize that lets you hide 'unnecessary' items from the WordPress backend.

SG Optimizer

The SG Optimizer is designed to link WordPress with all SiteGround Performance services.

Intuitive Custom Post Order

Intuitively, order items (Posts, Pages, and Custom Post Types, and Custom Taxonomies) using a drag and drop sortable JavaScript.

WP-DBManager

Manages your WordPress database.

Easy Theme and Plugin Upgrades

Easily upgrade your themes and plugins using zip files without removing the theme or plugin.

WP Editor

WP Editor is a plugin for WordPress that replaces the default plugin and theme editors.

Max Mega Menu

An easy to use mega menu plugin. Written the WordPress way.

Simple Custom Post Order

Order posts (posts, any custom post types) using a Drag and Drop Sortable JavaScript.

Theme Check

A simple and easy way to test your theme for all the latest WordPress standards.

White Label CMS

Customize dashboard panels and branding, remove menus, give editors access to widgets plus lots more.

Options Framework

The Options Framework Plugin makes it easy to include an options panel in any WordPress.

Head, Footer and Post Injections

Header and Footer plugin let you to add html code to the head and footer.

Easy Updates Manager

Manage all your WordPress updates, including individual updates, automatic updates, logs, and loads more.

CMB2

CMB2 is a metabox, custom fields, and forms library for WordPress that will blow your mind.

Post Duplicator

Creates functionality to duplicate any and all post types, including taxonomies & custom fields.

Revision Control

Revision Control allows finer control over the Post Revision system included with WordPress.

Advanced Code Editor

Enables syntax highlighting in the integrated themes and plugins source code editors with line numbers.

Menu Icons

Spice up your navigation menus with pretty icons, easily.

Advanced Automatic Updates

Adds extra options to WordPress' built-in Automatic Updates feature.

Category Order

The Order Categories plugin allows you to easily reorder your categories the way you want.

Portfolio Post Type

This plugin registers a custom post type for portfolio items.

CMS Tree Page View

Adds a tree view of all pages & custom posts.

Reveal IDs

What this plugin does is to reveal most removed IDs on admin pages, as it.

WordPress Database Reset

A plugin that allows you to skip the 5 minute installation and reset WordPress's database.

Optimize Database after Deleting Revisions

This plugin is a 'One Click' WordPress Database Cleaner / Optimizer.

Admin Columns

Manage and organize columns in the posts, users, comments and media lists in the WordPress admin panel.

Categories Images

The Categories Images Plugin allow you to add image with category or taxonomy.

WP Robots Txt

WP Robots Txt Allows you to edit the content of your robots.txt file.

Disable XML-RPC Pingback

Stops abuse of your site's XML-RPC by simply removing some methods used by attackers.

Disable XML-RPC

This plugin disables XML-RPC API in WordPress 3.5+, which is enabled by default.

Better Delete Revision

Better Delete Revision not only deletes redundant revisions of posts from your WordPress Database, it.

WP-Paginate

WP-Paginate is a simple and flexible pagination plugin which provides users with better navigation on.

Categories to Tags Converter

Convert existing categories to tags or tags to categories, selectively.

The WP Remote WordPress Plugin

WP Remote is a free web app that enables you to easily manage all of.

Post Grid, List for WordPress – Content Views

Display recent or any posts by category, tag, author, ID in responsive grid, list layout.

Bulk Delete

Bulk delete posts, pages, users, attachments and meta fields based on different conditions and filters.

WP Clean Up

WP Clean Up can help us to clean up the WordPress database by removing "revision"

WP Hide Post

Enables you to control the visibility of items on your blog by making posts/pages hidden.

Activity Log

The #1 Activity Log plugin helps you monitor & log all changes and activities on.

PHP Code for posts

Add PHP code to your WordPress posts, pages, custom post types and even sidebars using

WP Crontrol

WP Crontrol lets you view and control what's happening in the WP-Cron system.

SyntaxHighlighter Evolved

Easily post syntax-highlighted code to your site without having to modify the code at all.

Capability Manager Enhanced

A simple way to manage WordPress roles and capabilities.

Customizer Export/Import

Easily export or import your WordPress customizer settings!

Post Type Archive Link

Creates a metabox to the Appearance > Menu page to add custom post type archive

WP Htaccess Editor

Simple editor htaccess file without using FTP client.

WordPress REST API (Version 2)

Access your site's data through an easy-to-use HTTP REST API. (Version 2)

jQuery Updater

This plugin updates jQuery to the latest stable version on your website.

SSH SFTP Updater Support

"SSH SFTP Updater Support" is the easiest way to keep your WordPress installation up-to-date with

WP Updates Notifier

Sends email to notify you if there are any updates for your WordPress site.

WP-Sweep

WP-Sweep allows you to clean up unused, orphaned and duplicated data in your WordPress. It

AG Custom Admin

All-in-one tool for admin panel customization. Change almost everything: admin menu, dashboard, login page, admin

WP Admin UI Customize

Customize the management screen UI.

Ultimate Nofollow

Adds a checkbox in the insert link popup box for including rel="nofollow" in links as

Custom Field Suite

A custom fields management UI

Menu Social Icons

Add social icons to your WordPress menu items automatically.

Ultimate Category Excluder

Ultimate Category Excluder allows you to quickly and easily exclude categories from your front page,

Debug Bar

Adds a debug menu to the admin bar that shows query, cache, and other helpful

Meta Tag Manager

Easily add and manage custom meta tags to various parts of your site or on

File Manager

File Manager provides you ability to edit, delete, upload, download, copy and paste files and

Admin Menu Tree Page View

Get a tree view of all your pages directly in the admin menu. Search, edit,

Calculated Fields Form

Calculated Fields Form is a plugin for creating forms with dynamically calculated fields and display

Post Tags and Categories for Pages

Adds the built in WordPress categories and tags to your pages.

WP-Memory-Usage

Show up the PHP version, memory limit and current memory usage in the dashboard and

JQuery Accordion Menu Widget

Creates vertical accordion menus from any WordPress custom menu using jQuery. Add menus using either

109

Absolutely Glamorous Custom Admin

With this plugin you can easily customize WordPress admin panel, login page, admin menu, admin

WP Rollback

Rollback (or forward) any WordPress.org plugin or theme like a boss.

Widget Options

Get Better Control over your Widgets. Easily show or hide WordPress widgets on specified pages

WP Page Widget

Select widgets for each page / post / custom post type. For every single page

Show Current Template

A WordPress plugin which shows the current template file name, the current theme name and

Query Monitor

View debugging and performance information on database queries, hooks, conditionals, HTTP requests, redirects and more.

WordPress Infinite Scroll – Ajax Load More

The ultimate infinite scroll and lazy load solution for your WordPress powered website.

Export WordPress data to XML/CSV

WP All Export is an extremely powerful exporter that makes it easy to export any

If Menu

Display or hide menu items with user-defines rules

Duplicate Menu

Easily duplicate your WordPress menus with one click.

jQuery Smooth Scroll

Activate the plugin for smooth scrolling and smooth "back to top" feature.

Media File Renamer

Automatically rename files depending on Media titles dynamically + update links. Pro version has many

FV Top Level Categories

This is a fix of Top Level Categories plugin for WordPress 3.1. and above.

Site Unavailable & Under Construction Plugins (12)

WP Maintenance Mode

★★★★☆ (206)

Adds a splash page to your site that lets visitors know your site is down...

 Designmodo

 500,000+ active installations Tested with 4.8.4

WP Maintenance Mode

Adds a splash page to your site that lets visitors know your site is down.

Maintenance

Maintenance plugin allow WordPress site administrator close the website for maintenance, enable "503 Service temporarily unavailable", set a temporary page with authorization, which can be edited via the plugin settings.

Coming Soon Page & Maintenance Mode by SeedProd

The #1 Coming Soon Page, Under Construction & Maintenance Mode plugin for WordPress.

underConstruction

Creates a 'Coming Soon' page that will show for all users who are not logged in.

Ultimate Coming Soon Page

Creates a Coming Soon page or Launch page for your Website while it's under construction.

Under Construction / Maintenance Mode from Acurax

The easiest and feature-rich plugin to show under construction, coming soon, maintenance mode to visitors.

Under Construction

Display an Under Construction, Maintenance Mode or Landing Page that takes 5 seconds to setup.

Maintenance Mode

Maintenance mode with progress bar and responsive layout. Adds a responsive maintenance mode page to

Maintenance Mode

Very simple Maintenance Mode & Coming soon page using default WordPress markup with no ads

Coming soon, Maintenance Mode, Under Construction

Coming soon and Maintenance mode plugin is an awesome tool to show your website visitors

Minimal Coming Soon & Maintenance Mode

Simple & flexible Coming Soon & Maintenance Mode plugin – sets up in under a

WP Maintenance

Create and customize your maintenance page

Sitemap Plugins (11)

Google XML Sitemaps

★★★★★ (1,956)

This plugin will improve SEO by helping search enginess better index your site using sitemaps.

👤 Arne Brachhold

📊 2+ million active installations Ⓦ Tested with 4.8.4

Google XML Sitemaps

This plugin will generate a special XML sitemap which will help search engines like Google, Bing, Yahoo and Ask.com to better index your blog.

PS Auto Sitemap

Auto generator of a customizable and designed sitemap page.

Better WordPress Google XML Sitemaps (support Sitemap Index, Multi-site and Google News)

A WordPress XML Sitemap plugin that comes with support for Sitemap Index, Multi-site and Google.

WP Sitemap Page

Add a sitemap on any of your page using the simple shortcode [wp_sitemap_page].

XML Sitemap & Google News feeds

XML and Google News Sitemaps to feed the hungry spiders. Multisite, WP Super Cache, and Polylang.

Google Sitemap by BestWebSoft

Generate and add XML sitemap to WordPress website. Help search engines index your blog.

Google XML Sitemap for Videos

This plugin will help you generate Google Video Sitemaps (XML) for your WordPress blog.

Simple Sitemap

The simplest responsive HTML sitemap available for WordPress! No setup required. Flexible customization options available.

HTML Page Sitemap

Adds an HTML (Not XML) sitemap of your pages (not posts) by entering the shortcode

WP Realtime Sitemap

A sitemap plugin to make it easier for your site to show all your pages,

Simple Wp Sitemap

An easy sitemap plugin that adds both an xml and an html sitemap to your

Slider Plugins (10)

MetaSlider

 (412)

Easy to use WordPress slider plugin.
Create SEO-optimized responsive
slideshows with Nivo Slider, Flex Slider,....

 Team Updraft

 800,000+ active installations    Tested with 4.9.1

Meta Slider

The most popular WordPress slider plugin. Creating slideshows
with Meta Slider is fast and easy. Simply select images from your
WordPress Media Library, drag and drop them into place, set slide
captions, links and SEO fields all from one page.

Slider – Image Slider

Slider Huge-IT is an awesome WordPress Slider Plugin with many
nice features.

Master Slider – Responsive Touch Slider

The most advanced responsive and HTML5 WordPress slider plugin
with touch swipe navigation that works.

Slider by Soliloquy – Responsive Image Slider for WordPress

The best WordPress slider plugin. Drag & Drop responsive slider
builder that helps you create.

Easing Slider

The easiest way to create sliders with WordPress.

Smart Slider 3

Responsive slider plugin to create beautiful sliders in the next generation visual editor.

Cyclone Slider 2

An easy-to-use and customizable slideshow plugin. For both casual users and expert developers.

Meteor Slides

Easily create responsive slideshows with WordPress that are mobile friendly and simple to customize.

Slider by WD – Responsive Slider for WordPress

Slider WD plugin is the perfect slider solution for WordPress.

Slide Anything – Responsive Content / HTML Slider and Carousel

Create responsive carousels or sliders where the content for each slide can be anything you

Social Media & Sharing Plugins (47)

AddToAny Share Buttons

★★★★☆ (685)

Share buttons for WordPress including the AddToAny sharing button, Facebook, Twitter, Google+, Pinterest, WhatsApp, many...

 AddToAny

400,000+ active installations 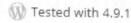 Tested with 4.9.1

AddToAny Share Buttons

Share buttons for WordPress including the AddToAny sharing button, Facebook, Twitter, Google+, Pinterest, WhatsApp, and many more.

Instagram Feed

Display beautifully clean, customizable, and responsive feeds from multiple Instagram accounts.

Simple Social Icons

This plugin allows you to insert social icons in any widget area.

Share Buttons by AddThis

Increase social traffic to your website with WordPress share buttons.

Custom Facebook Feed

Display a completely customizable, responsive and search engine crawlable version of your Facebook feed on your website.

NextScripts: Social Networks Auto-Poster

Automatically publishes blogposts to profiles/pages/groups on Facebook, Twitter, Instagram, Google+, Pinterest, LinkedIn, Blogger, Tumblr, and more.

Social Media Widget

Adds links to all of your social media and sharing site profiles.

Free Tools to Automate Your Site Growth

Free and easy way to double your email subscribers, plus sharing tools to double your traffic.

WP Instagram Widget

WP Instagram widget is a no fuss WordPress widget to showcase your latest Instagram pics.

Simple Share Buttons Adder

A simple plugin that enables you to add share buttons to all of your posts.

Social Media Feather | social media sharing

Lightweight, modern looking and effective social media sharing and profile buttons and icons.

Shareaholic | share buttons, related posts, social analytics & more

World's leading all-in-one Content Amplification Platform that helps grow your site traffic, engagement, conversions & more.

Facebook Like Box Widget

Facebook Like Box Widget is a social plugin that enables Facebook Page owners to attract.

Easy Facebook Like Box – Custom Facebook Feed – Auto PopUp

Easy Facebook like box WordPress plugin allows to display custom Facebook feed.

oAuth Twitter Feed for Developers

Twitter API 1.1 compliant plugin that provides a function to get an array of tweet.

Facebook Widget

This widget adds a Simple Facebook page Like Widget into your WordPress website Sidebar.

Social Share WordPress Plugin – AccessPress Social Share

Share your site urls in most popular social medias and show share counts on your.

Instagram Slider Widget

Instagram Slider Widget is a responsive slider widget that shows 12 latest images from a.

Social Icons WordPress Plugin – AccessPress Social Icons

Add social media icons on your site | select from pre-designed sets or upload your.

Social Media and Share Icons (Ultimate Social Media)

Easy to use social media plugin which adds social media icons to your website with.

WP to Twitter

Posts a Twitter update when you update your WordPress blog or add a link.

Instagram Feed WD – Instagram Gallery for WordPress

Instagram Feed WD is a user-friendly plugin to display user or hashtag-based Instagram feeds as.

Facebook Conversion Pixel

In 2016, Facebook transitioned to an updated version of the Custom Audience and Conversion pixels.

Facebook

Facebook Like Box plugin comes with Facebook Like Box Widget & Shortcode.

Social Media

Super-easy to use social media plugin which adds social media icons to your website with.

Social Media Share Buttons | MashShare

Social Media Share Buttons for Twitter, Facebook and other social networks.

Tracking Code Manager

A plugin to manage ALL your tracking code and conversion pixels.

Social Media Flying Icons | Floating Social Media Icon .

Social Media Plugin with 30+ Social Media Icon Styles,Easy Configuration,Social Media Widget,Icon Animation,Drag Reorder,Highly Customizable.

Social Counter for WordPress – AccessPress Social Counter

A plugin to display your social accounts fans, subscribers and followers number on your website.

Facebook Like Box

Facebook like box plugin will help you to display Facebook like box on your wesite,

Feed Them Social – Facebook, Instagram, Twitter, Vine, Pinterest, etc

Custom feeds for Facebook Pages, Groups, Events, Album Photos, Videos & Covers, Twitter, Vine, Instagram,

Easy Social Icons

Upload your own social media icons or choose from font-awesome. Use widget|shortcode to place icons

Social Count Plus

Displays your number of followers from Facebook, Google+, Instagram, Twitch, Twitter and several other social

Facebook Pixel by PixelYourSite – Events, WooCommerce & Easy Digital Downloads

Insert the new Facebook Pixel on WordPress, add Events, enjoy superb WooCommerce & EDD Facebook

I Recommend This

This plugin allows your visitors to simply like/recommend your posts instead of comment on it.

Social Share Buttons – Social Pug

Social share buttons with style that will increase your social shares and user interaction with

Social Media Widget by Acurax

Social Media Widget Plugin, A Simple Social Icon Widget To Show Essential Social Media Icons

Facebook Auto Publish

Publish posts automatically to Facebook page or profile.

Lightweight Social Icons

Looking to add simple social icons to your widget areas? Choose the size and color

Facebook Button by BestWebSoft

Add Facebook Follow, Like, and Share buttons to WordPress posts, pages, and widgets.

Rotating Tweets (Twitter widget and shortcode)

Twitter widget and shortcode to show your latest tweets one at a time an animated

Pinterest Pin It Button On Image Hover And Post

Pin Your WordPress Blog Posts Pages Images With Pinterest Plugin

Social Icons Widget by WPZOOM

Social Icons Widget to displays links to social sharing websites. Supports more than 80 sites

Social Warfare

The most beautiful, lightning fast social media sharing buttons built to boost shares and drive

jQuery Pin It Button for Images

Highlights images on hover and adds a Pinterest "Pin It" button over them for easy

Custom Share Buttons with Floating Sidebar

Social Share Buttons

Table & Database Plugins (2)

TablePress

★★★★★ (3,112)

Embed beautiful and feature-rich tables into your posts and pages, without having to write code.

Tobias Bäthge

600,000+ active installations   ⓦ Tested with 4.9.1

TablePress

Embed beautiful and feature-rich tables into your posts and pages, without having to write code.

Pricing Tables WordPress Plugin – Easy Pricing Tables

Pricing Table Plugin – Easy Pricing Tables Lets You Create A Beautiful, Responsive Pricing Table

Terms, Site Info, and Cookie Plugins (8)

Cookie Notice by dFactory

Cookie Notice allows you to elegantly inform users that your site uses cookies.

Cookie Law Info

A simple way to show how your website complies with the EU Cookie Law.

Auto Terms of Service and Privacy Policy

Put your own details into a modified version of Automattic's "Terms of Service" and "Privacy Policy."

Cookie Consent

The only cookie consent plugin you'll ever need.

EU Cookie Law

EU Cookie Law informs users that your site uses cookies, with option to lock scripts.

Asesor de Cookies para normativa española

Este plugin le va a facilitar la confección de la política de cookies para.

Italy Cookie Choices (for EU Cookie Law)

Italy Cookie Choices allows you to easily comply with the european cookie law and block

Cookies for Comments

Sets a cookie on a random URL that is then checked when a comment is

User Management Plugins (10)

User Role Editor

User Role Editor WordPress plugin makes user roles and capabilities changing easy.

WP User Avatar

Use any image from your WordPress Media Library as a custom user avatar.

Nav Menu Roles

Hide custom menu items based on user roles.

WP-UserOnline

Enable you to display how many users are online on your WordPress blog with detailed

Simple Local Avatars

Adds an avatar upload field to user profiles. Generates requested sizes on demand just like.

User Switching

Instant switching between user accounts in WordPress.

Edit Author Slug

Allows an admin (or capable user) to edit the author slug of a user, and.

WPFront User Role Editor

Easily allows you to manage WordPress user roles. You can create, edit, delete and manage.

User Access Manager

With the "User Access Manager"-plugin you can manage the access to your posts, pages and

Remove Dashboard Access

Allows you to disable Dashboard access for users of a specific role or capability. Disallowed

Visual Editor, Page Builder, CSS, & Theme Plugins (43)

TinyMCE Advanced

 (264)

Extends and enhances TinyMCE, the WordPress Visual Editor.

 Andrew Ozz

2+ million active installations Tested with 4.9.1

TinyMCE Advanced

Extends and enhances TinyMCE, the WordPress Visual Editor.

Black Studio TinyMCE Widget

The visual editor widget for WordPress.

Redux Framework

Redux is a simple, truly extensible and fully responsive options framework for WordPress themes.

Genesis Simple Edits

This plugin creates a new Genesis settings page that allows you to modify the post-info (byline), post-meta, and footer area on any Genesis theme.

WP Retina 2x

Make your website look beautiful and crisp on modern displays by creating and displaying retina images.

Page Builder by SiteOrigin

Build responsive page layouts using the widgets you know and love using this simple drag and drop editor.

SiteOrigin CSS

SiteOrigin CSS plugin.

Beaver Builder – WordPress Page Builder

The best drag and drop WordPress Page Builder.

Child Theme Configurator

When using the Customizer is not enough – Create a child theme from your installed.

AddQuicktag

This plugin makes it easy to add Quicktags to the html – and visual-editor.

Spacer

Adds a spacer button to the WYSIWYG visual editor.

Kirki

The ultimate toolkit for theme developers using the WordPress Customizer.

Responsive Menu

Highly customisable Responsive Menu plugin with 150+ options.

OptionTree

Theme Options UI Builder for WordPress. A simple way to create & save Theme Options.

Genesis Simple Hooks

This plugin creates a new Genesis settings page that allows you to insert code.

Cryout Serious Theme Settings

This plugin is designed to inter-operate with our Mantra, Parabola, Tempera, Nirvana themes to restore.

One-Click Child Theme

Adds a Theme option to any active theme allowing you to make a child theme.

Elementor Page Builder

The most advanced frontend drag & drop page builder.

Unyson

A simple and easy way to build a powerful website.

WP Responsive Menu

WP Responsive Menu turns your WordPress menu to a highly customizable sliding responsive menu.

SiteOrigin Widgets by CodeLights

Flexible high-end shortcodes and widgets. Responsive, modern, SEO-optimized and easy-to-use. Also can work without SiteOrigin.

Scroll Back To Top

This plugin will add a button that allows users to scroll smoothly to the top

Page Builder: Live Composer – drag and drop website builder (visual front-end site editor)

Front-end page builder for WordPress with drag and drop editing. Build PRO responsive websites and

Simple Custom CSS and JS

Easily add Custom CSS or JS to your website with an awesome editor.

WP PageNavi Style

Adds a more styling options to Wp-PageNavi WordPress plugin.

Genesis Title Toggle

Turn on/off page titles on a per page basis, and set sitewide defaults from Theme

Any Mobile Theme Switcher

This Plugin detects mobile browser and display the theme as the setting done from admin.

Advanced Image Styles

Adjust an image's margins and border with ease in the Visual editor.

Child Themify

Create child themes at the click of a button.

Forget About Shortcode Buttons

A visual way to add CSS buttons in the post editor screen and to your

Animate It!

Add cool CSS3 animations to your content.

Sticky Menu (or Anything!) on Scroll

Sticky Menu (Or Anything!) On Scroll will let you choose any element on your page

What The File

What The File is the best tool to find out what template parts are used

WPFront Scroll Top

WPFront Scroll Top plugin allows the visitor to easily scroll back to the top of

Fourteen Colors

Not a big fan of green and black? Love the layout of Twenty Fourteen, but

Nested Pages

Nested Pages provides a drag and drop interface for managing pages & posts in the

Insert Html Snippet

Add HTML, CSS and javascript code to your pages and posts easily using shortcodes.

Simple Custom CSS

Add Custom CSS to your WordPress site without any hassles.

WP Add Custom CSS

Add custom css to the whole website and to specific posts and pages.

Simple CSS

Add CSS to your website through an admin editor, the Customizer or a metabox for

MCE Table Buttons

Adds table editing controls to the visual content editor (TinyMCE).

Re-add text underline and justify

In WordPress 4.7, the core developper team decided to make various changes in the editor

Page Builder: KingComposer – Free Drag and Drop page builder by King-Theme

Lightweight and extremely powerful Page Builder. Allow you to easily create pages like a true

Website Performance & Speed Plugins (11)

Autoptimize

Autoptimize speeds up your website and helps you save bandwidth by aggregating and minimizing JS.

P3 (Plugin Performance Profiler)

See which plugins are slowing down your site.

Compress JPEG & PNG images

Speed up your website. Optimize your JPEG and PNG images automatically with TinyPNG.

ShortPixel Image Optimizer

Speed up your website and boost your SEO by compressing old & new images and

Cloudflare

All of Cloudflare's performance and security benefits in a simple one-click install.

Better WordPress Minify

Allows you to combine and minify your CSS and JS files to improve page load times.

Lazy Load

Lazy load images to improve page load times and server bandwidth.

Remove Query Strings From Static Resources

Remove query strings from static resources like CSS & JS files.

BJ Lazy Load

Lazy loading for images and iframes makes your site load faster and saves bandwidth. Uses

WP Performance Score Booster

Speed-up page load times and improve website scores in services like PageSpeed, YSlow, Pingdom and

a3 Lazy Load

Use a3 Lazy Load for images, videos, iframes. Instantly improve your sites load time and

Widget & Sidebar Plugins (35)

Widget Importer & Exporter

Import and export your widgets.

Display Widgets

Simply hide widgets on specified pages. Adds checkboxes to each widget to either show or not.

Custom Sidebars – Dynamic Widget Area Manager

Flexible sidebars for custom widget configurations on every page, post and custom post type.

SiteOrigin Widgets Bundle

The SiteOrigin widget bundle gives you a collection of widgets that you can use and customize. All the widgets are built on our powerful framework, giving you advanced forms, unlimited colors and 1500+ icons.

Widget Logic

Widget Logic lets you control on which pages widgets appear using WP's conditional tags.

Image Widget

Image Widget is a simple plugin that uses the native WordPress media manager to add image widgets to your site.

Contact Widgets

Beautifully display social media and contact information on your website with these simple widgets.

Widget Logic

Widget Logic lets you control on which pages widgets appear using WP's conditional tags.

WooSidebars

WooSidebars adds functionality to display different widgets in a sidebar.

PHP Code Widget

Like the Text widget, but also allows working PHP code to be inserted.

Exec-PHP

The Exec-PHP plugin executes PHP code in posts, pages and text widgets.

Q2W3 Fixed Widget

Fixes positioning of the selected widgets, when the page is scrolled down.

Widget CSS Classes

Add custom classes and ids plus first, last, even, odd, and numbered classes to your site.

WP Tab Widget

WP Tab Widget is the AJAXified plugin which loads content by demand, and thus it.

Category Posts Widget

Adds a widget that shows the most recent posts from a single category.

Dynamic Widgets

Dynamic Widgets gives you full control on which pages a widget will display.

Simple Image Widget

A simple widget that makes it a breeze to add images to your sidebars.

amr shortcode any widget

Insert a widget or multiple widgets or a entire widget area (sidebar) into a page.

SMK Sidebar Generator

This plugin generates as many sidebars as you need.

Widgets on Pages

The easy way to Add Widgets or Sidebars to Posts and Pages using shortcodes or.

Enhanced Text Widget

An enhanced version of the text widget that supports Text, HTML, CSS, JavaScript, Flash, Shortcodes.

Widget Context

Show or hide widgets on specific posts, pages or sections of your site.

Simple Page Sidebars

Easily assign custom, widget-enabled sidebars to any page.

Widget Shortcode

Adds [widget] shortcode which enables you to output widgets anywhere you like.

Genesis Simple Sidebars

This plugin allows you to create multiple, dynamic widget areas, and assign those widget areas

Widget Content Blocks

Edit widget content using the default WordPress visual editor and media uploading functionality.

Ultimate Posts Widget

The ultimate widget for displaying posts, custom post types or sticky posts with an array

Awesome Weather Widget

Finally beautiful weather widgets for your beautiful site.

Content Blocks (Custom Post Widget)

This plugin enables you to edit and display Content Blocks in a sidebar widget or

Content Aware Sidebars – Unlimited Widget Areas

Display widget areas and custom sidebars on any post, page, category etc. Supports bbPress, BuddyPress,

PHP Text Widget

Executes PHP code on WordPress default Text Widget

Flexi Pages Widget

A highly configurable WordPress sidebar widget to list pages and sub-pages. User friendly widget control

Flexible Posts Widget

An advanced posts display widget with many options. Display posts in your sidebars any way

Video Sidebar Widgets

A collection of sidebar widgets for displaying Flash Videos from 14 video sharing networks.

Livemesh SiteOrigin Widgets

A collection of premium quality widgets for use in any widgetized area or in SiteOrigin

Widgets for SiteOrigin

A collection of highly customizable and thoughtfully crafted widgets. Built on top of the SiteOrigin

YouTube & Video Plugins (8)

YouTube

YouTube Embed WordPress Plugin. Embed a responsive video, YouTube channel gallery, playlist gallery, or live.

YouTube Embed

An incredibly fast, simple, yet powerful, method of embedding YouTube videos into your WordPress site.

YouTube Widget Responsive

Share your channel with YouTube button subscribe.

WP Video Lightbox

Very easy to use WordPress lightbox plugin to display YouTube and Vimeo videos in an.

Gallery – Video Gallery and YouTube Gallery

Gallery Video plugin was created and specifically designed to show video links in unusual splendid

YouTube Channel Gallery

Show a YouTube video and a gallery of thumbnails for a YouTube channel.

FV Flowplayer Video Player

WordPress's most reliable, easy to use and feature-rich video player. Supports responsive design, HTML5, playlists

Featured Video Plus

Add Featured Videos to your posts and pages. Works like magic with most themes which

I Invite You to Subscribe, Like, and Stay Connected for Additional Content

→ Chadtennant.com / YouTube / Facebook / LinkedIn

To learn of my new books, please join my new book club (https://www.chadtennant.com/new-book-club/) and follow my Amazon author page.

Please take a few seconds to leave a review on Amazon. Your thoughts are appreciated!

Made in the USA
San Bernardino, CA
12 April 2018